D0816162

Have You Heard From The Lord Lately?

DAVE WILLIAMS

Have You Heard From The Lord Lately?

Learning To Hear And Know The Voice Of God

DAVE WILLIAMS

Have You Heard From The Lord Lately?
Learning To Hear And Know The Voice of God

All rights reserved. No part of this publication may be reproduced, stored in a retrieval system, or transmitted in any form or by any means — electronic, mechanical, photocopy, recording, or any other — except for brief quotations in printed reviews, without prior permission of the publisher.

Unless otherwise noted, Scripture quotations are taken from the New King James Version of the Bible.

Copyright © 2002 by David R. Williams

ISBN 0-938020-02-1

First Printing 2002

Cover Design: Gerard R. Jones

Published by:

DECAPOLIS
PUBLISHING

Printed in the United States of America

Books by Dave Williams

ABCs of Success and Happiness
AIDS Plague
Art of Pacesetting Leadership
Beauty of Holiness
Christian Job Hunter's Handbook
Desires of Your Heart
Depression, Cave of Torment
Genuine Prosperity, The Power To Get Wealth
Getting To Know Your Heavenly Father
Gifts That Shape Your Life And Change Your World
Grand Finale Revival
Grief and Mourning
Growing Up in Our Father's Family
Have You Heard From the Lord Lately?
How to Be a High Performance Believer
          in Low Octane Days
How You Can Be Filled With The Holy Spirit
Laying On of Hands
Lonely in the Midst of a Crowd
Miracle Results of Fasting
The New Life . . . The Start of Something Wonderful
The Pastor's Pay
Questions I Have Answered
Patient Determination
Revival Power of Music
Remedy for Worry and Tension
Road To Radical Riches
Secret of Power With God
Seven Signposts on the Road to Spiritual Maturity
Slain in the Spirit — Real or Fake?
Somebody Out There Needs You
Success Principles From the Lips of Jesus
Supernatural Soulwinning
Thirty-Six Minutes with the Pastor
Understanding Spiritual Gifts
What To Do If You Miss The Rapture
World Beyond — The Mysteries of Heaven

My special thanks to Marjie Knight for her literary skills in helping me get this book on paper and in print.

Thanks, Marjie!

Contents

"If we want to know what our future holds, we can ask and the Holy Spirit will tell us."

Does God Still Speak In Supernatural Ways?

Not too long ago news headlines flashed around the world: "2000 Too Grand!" Extravagant light shows and spectacular fireworks lit the skies from Sydney, Australia to Hong Kong to New York City to London to Paris and Moscow welcoming the new Millennium. Amidst all the revelry lingered cautious fear of Y2K predictions of computer mayhem and terrorist threats, war and rumors of war. In spite of all the wild partying and apparent merriment, the future was uncertain. No one could say for sure what might be about to happen.

As you read the headlines of the newspaper or watched the worldwide celebrations on TV, did you find yourself asking, "Lord, what does this new century, this new millennium, hold for me and my family?" Now let me ask you this. Did God answer your question? Better yet, did you expect or believe it was possible to receive an answer from Him? How you answer these questions indicates whether you believe God still speaks in supernatural ways to His people today.

Take Sharla, for example, a young Christian minister who was preparing to travel back to Singapore after a week of ministry near Boston. Less than fifteen hours before her scheduled flight to Los Angeles, where she would connect with another flight to Singapore, the Lord spoke to her as she prayed, "Sharla, reschedule your flight. Go back next week. I want to give you some rest."

"But, Lord, I want to get back to Singapore," Sharla protested.

"Sharla, reschedule your flight," the inner voice persisted.

Confident that the Lord had spoken to her, she called her agent to reschedule her upcoming flight to Los Angeles. The next morning, Sharla slept in until almost ten in the morning. She felt rested and refreshed.

Then the news. Her originally scheduled flight, United Airlines Flight 175, from Boston, Massachu-

setts, to Los Angeles, California, was hijacked by terrorists. Two pilots, seven flight attendants and 56
passengers were on board. At 9:03 a.m. United Airlines Flight 175 from Boston crashed into the south
tower of the World Trade Center and exploded, killing everyone on board and hundreds of others in the
building.

Sharla's heart raced as she heard the news, realizing that she was originally scheduled on that flight.
Her heart cried for those whose lives were snuffed
out in this tragedy, yet grateful that she had listened
to the voice of God.

Lisa Wheeler is another example. She traveled
extensively in her business flying around the country. As she was spending time in regular prayer, the
Lord gently spoke to her, telling her to stay in town
during September and to take no business flights.
Now she knows why. She may have been in Boston,
or New York, or some other city on that fateful day.
She may have been on one of the four airliners that
crashed by the hand of terrorists on September 11,
2001.

The list goes on and on concerning those to whom
God spoke.

Tens of thousands of copies of my book entitled
Grief and Mourning were shipped to ministry stations in New York right after the tragedy. They helped

pastors and ministry leaders in helping the thousands of people who would never see their loved ones again. Pastors began to write to me with story after story how God had spoken to people to stay away from the Trade Center that day. God does speak. The question is, are we listening?

In this tumultuous, rapidly changing and increasingly volatile global economy and culture, everyone wants to know what lies ahead for this and future generations. Technology is changing the way we live faster than we can even comprehend. The information superhighway — the Internet — can flash a message around the world eight times a second. Yet, with all this information and technology at their fingertips, people are still asking that age-old question, "What does my future hold?"

The reason so many people, including many Christians, never get a valid answer to their question fits into one of three categories. First and foremost, many don't believe God holds the answer and they go looking for the answer in all the wrong places. Secondly, others don't believe He will speak to them so they don't expect an answer. Thirdly, they just simply don't ask Him. Whatever category people fit into, they have a burning *need* to know what the future has in store for them, and many go to great lengths to search out an answer.

Because people have not turned to God, they have turned to other sources of information such as fortune-tellers, ouija boards or horoscopes. Others call 1-900-PSYCHIC or, as one evangelist puts it, 1-900-DIAL-A-DEMON! It seems that everything related to the supernatural has been relegated to the dark world of demons and the occult. That is why we are seeing psychics and fortune-tellers putting signs outside their houses and setting up shop in malls around the country.

The occult has come out of the closet. Bookstores are filled with best-selling books on everything from New Age to Satanism. Movies such as "The Blair Witch Project" shot to the top of the ticket-sales chart one week after opening. Television programs such as "Sabrina, the Teenage Witch," "Buffy, the Vampire Slayer" and "Charmed" blatantly tout the power of witchcraft as they lure our young people into thinking this is normal and fun. The US military allows the practice of Wicca, often referred to as white witchcraft, on military bases cloaked in the guise of "religion." Mind science cults are popping up everywhere promising that followers can discover their destiny in the cults' various courses and methods. Many well-known Hollywood celebrities and high-level political and business leaders are involved in these cults and practices. We could go on and on, but the point is, everything related to the supernatural that is being practiced in the devil's camp is simply a counterfeit of the true, supernatural power of God.

God has promised us a future, and He had a plan in place for each one of us before time began. God didn't create the world, wind it up and take off saying, "Do the best you can, and I'll be back someday." God is right here with us just as He was with Moses and Abraham and the apostles of the New Testament.

> And the LORD, he *it is* that doth go before thee; he will be with thee, he will not fail thee, neither forsake thee: fear not, neither be dismayed.
>
> — Deuteronomy 31:8 (KJV)
>
> for he hath said, I will never leave thee, nor forsake thee.
>
> — Hebrews 13:5b (KJV)

God is still in the miracle business just as He was in the days of the early church in the book of Acts. God never changes. David spoke of it as he wrote the Psalms in the Old Testament, as did the writer of the book of Hebrews in the New Testament.

> But you remain the same, and your years will never end.
>
> — Psalm 102:27 (NIV)

But you remain the same, and your years will
never end.

— Hebrews 1:12b (NIV)

Jesus Christ is the same yesterday and today
and forever.

— Hebrews 13:8 (NIV)

When Jesus physically left this earth to return to
His Father in Heaven, He sent His Spirit to us to comfort us, guide us and tell us things to come. So, if we
want to know what our future holds, we can ask and
the Holy Spirit will tell us.

And I will pray the Father, and He will give you
another Helper, that He may abide with you forever — the Spirit of truth, whom the world cannot receive, because it neither sees Him nor
knows Him; but you know Him, for He dwells
with you and will be in you.

— John 14:16, 17

However, when He, the Spirit of truth, has come,
He will guide you into all truth; for He will not
speak on His own authority, but whatever He
hears He will speak; and He will tell you things
to come.

— John 16:13

I see something in those early New Testament
Christians I want back. They had an ear to Heaven.
They were listening for the Holy Spirit. As a result,
the book of Acts pulsates with supernatural events

and supernatural phenomena. By the time you get to the eighth chapter, Philip has cast out unclean spirits and the occult was put out of business! Simon the Sorcerer, the head of the New Age movement back then, was clobbered by the Gospel of Jesus. In the ninth chapter, Saul — the judge, juror and executioner of the Christians — *heard* the voice of God when a bright light shone down on him from Heaven on the road to Damascus.

God also spoke in separate visions both to Saul and Ananias, that Ananias was to come and pray for Saul. By the tenth chapter, people have been raised from the dead, apostles' shadows have healed people, and a man who had been crippled for 40 years received a creative miracle. Encounters with angels were commonplace, and supernatural transportation was faster than today's space shuttle. How would our society or even in the church interpret these today?

When anything supernatural takes place today, many people say, "That's too weird," or "way out there." Angel books are popular, but most of them talk about spirit guides that are really dark angels rather than godly angels from Heaven. Dreams are most often attributed to eating too much pizza before bed or just coincidence. Visions and trances are thought to be something paranormal from the dark side. When someone says the Lord told him or her to do something, the most common reaction is, "Yeah, right!"

I believe we are living in the last days. I'm not predicting Jesus is coming back today or tomorrow or next Friday, but I know He is coming back *soon*. You can interpret that any way you want, but it is obvious these are perilous days. I believe the supernatural power demonstrated in the book of Acts is as much for us today as it was for the early Christians. That is a fact the body of Christ needs to grasp.

In 1988 Paul Cain, a humble man called of God to the office of a prophet and thought by some to be a modern day Elijah, called John Wimber, the founder of the Vineyard churches, and said, "I'm coming to California to see you because I have a word from the Lord for you."

John didn't know Paul Cain at that time and cautiously asked, "Will the Lord give me a sign you are really a man of God, and your word is from Him?"

Paul said, "Yes, on the day I arrive there will be an earthquake in your area."

John said, "Will this be the big one we've all been waiting for?"

Paul replied, "No. On the day after I leave there will be a massive earthquake elsewhere in the world."

Paul Cain arrived in California on December 3, 1988 and a moderate earthquake hit Pasadena and Anaheim that day. Paul delivered his word to John Wimber concerning the future of the Vineyard churches. He left California on December 7, 1988. On December 8, 1988 a massive earthquake devastated Soviet Armenia, and reports were broadcast on TV and in all the newspapers.[1]

God *does still speak* in supernatural ways to those who have ears to hear. That is why I have written this book. It is time to dispel the church traditions that for centuries have robbed God's people of walking in and demonstrating the power of the Holy Spirit. It is time to recognize the different ways in which God speaks today. It is time to reclaim the intimacy with God of the early church, which allowed believers to know His ways and character and operate in His power. It is time to tune our ears to the Spirit of God.

You and I have had the awesome privilege of crossing the time bridge into the new Millennium. With that privilege comes a responsibility to be ambassadors for Christ. In doing so, we can change the course of history by preparing hearts to release a new passion for God, setting the body of Christ on fire to enforce what Jesus did at Calvary. This can only be done by the power of the Holy Spirit.

Whether you walk in that power and fulfill your destiny on this earth depends on *hearing* the voice of God and *doing* what He says without question and without hesitation. It is the difference between life and death — eternal life in God's kingdom or eternal damnation in Satan's kingdom. That may sound harsh but it is truth spoken in love. It is my desire that you have ears to hear what the Spirit is saying today to take you into your promised future.

"How many have missed God's very best, most exciting, and fascinating adventures because they had to figure it all out first?"

Chapter 1

A Fascinating Adventure

How would you like your life to be a fascinating adventure? Every time I've heard a major word from the Lord, my life, thereafter, became a fascinating adventure. When we were getting ready to build Mount Hope Church in Lansing, Michigan, the Lord spoke to me and said, "Don't go to the bank and borrow money." When I heard that word, I knew I was in for a fascinating adventure. A word from the Lord can bring your life into a state of adventure.

God Spoke Through A Ford!

I had my Sunday morning message prepared one Saturday evening at 6:30 p.m. I was ready to preach an exciting, fiery message titled, "What Killed the Church!" At 6:35 p.m. a musical jingle rang through my mind that sounded like the jingle from the TV commercial, "Have you driven a Ford lately," but instead it was saying, "Have you heard from the Lord lately?" The Lord began ministering to my heart and said, "Ask my people this question: 'Have you heard from the Lord lately?'"

The Lord spoke through a Ford when he said, "Have you heard from the Lord lately?" It kept running through my mind and I said, "Okay, Lord, I will ask your people that question on Sunday morning." At that point I really had no idea what I would add to that question to make a message, but simply trusted that He knew best and would give me the message when I was obedient.

As the jingle kept ringing in my head, I began to think how life becomes an adventure when we learn to hear from the Lord. I was drawn to an event in the life of Abram before he was renamed, "Abraham." Abram lived with his family in an area of the world now known as Iraq. This was 1800 years before Jesus was born. Let's look at what the Bible says.

> Now the Lord had said unto Abram, Get thee out of thy country and from thy kindred and from thy father's house, unto a land that I will shew thee.
>
> — Genesis 12:1 (KJV)

Notice God *spoke* directly to Abram and Abram *heard* Him. God gave Abram an instruction and then

told him what would happen when he obeyed as we
read in the next three verses.

> And I will make of thee a great nation, and I will
> bless thee, and make thy name great; and thou
> shalt be a blessing. And I will bless them that
> bless thee, and curse them that curseth thee: and
> in thee shall all families of the earth be blessed.
> So Abram departed, as the Lord had spoken unto
> him.
>
> — Genesis 12:2-4 (KJV)

We know the rest of the story. God gave Abram a
word, and when Abram obeyed, his life became a
fascinating adventure.

The Adventure Begins

In the early growing years at Mount Hope Church,
I saw excitement and enthusiasm building. In my first
year we had given approximately $3,500 to missions.
I wanted to know where the church was headed so I
went down to my basement to pray. As I knelt down
on a little platform I built to keep from getting wet
from the damp floor, I began to ask the Lord, "Where
is our church going?" I prayed in the Spirit, sang and
talked to God. Then I got quiet in case the Lord
wanted to speak something to me. In that quiet moment the furnace kicked on with a "whoosh," and in
my heart, I sensed the Holy Spirit saying, "What's
happening in your church right now is like a pilot
light compared to what's going to happen. I'm going

to open the main gas valve. The revival fires are going to burn and spill over into other nations. I will make your church a blessing to many nations and many denominations, and the blessing I gave to Abraham I will give to your church as well." Those were the words that came to me from the Lord at that time.

In the next 20 short years, mission giving at Mount Hope went from thirty-five hundred dollars to 2.5 million for the sake of world outreach. We are influencing churches all over America and touching missionaries' lives around the globe. Here's an example:

I had just finished speaking at a missions conference in Fort Wayne, Indiana, when a missionary stood up to speak. He was not called upon to speak and it was probably inappropriate for him to do so, but he said, "I've got to say something to this group. I've never been more proud in all my life of what God has done at Mount Hope Church. They've supported me for twenty-three years."

He then went on and explained some of the things Mount Hope had done in the world that even we didn't know about. Testimony that we've become a blessing to many nations and denominations. This missionary verified that when we listen to the Lord, our lives become fascinating adventures.

What Are You Listening To?

When we listen to other voices our lives become bored, troubled and perplexed. What do you listen to? Do you listen to gossip? Do you listen to slander from the mouth of the person who doesn't know what he's talking about? Do you listen to music that is not exalting the Lord? What is it that you listen to? Is your life a fascinating adventure or is it troubled and boring? God loves to talk to us about even the simplest things.

God Is Always Listening

When Chuck Smith was pastoring in Arizona, he had a 15-minute radio program. On one of his programs he told this story. Driving down the road one day, he was tuning into his radio program but the sound was intermittent and filled with a lot of static.

Not even realizing that the Lord would respond back to him, he said, "Lord, what's wrong with that radio?" Just then, a picture came to his mind of a little speaker with a loose wire in the trunk of the car hooked up under the back window on the inside of the car. He'd never seen such a picture before in his life but he thought he'd check it out. He pulled over to the side of the road, crawled into the trunk of the car, pulled the cardboard down and looked. There he saw a speaker up under the back window of the car and, sure enough, it had a loose wire just as he had envisioned.

He tightened the wire, twisted around, climbed out of the trunk and tried the radio. It worked perfectly. He was so excited that God had spoken to him he turned the radio off and said, "Oh Lord, I'll just listen to you."[1]

A Member of God's Family

You came into the family of God when you decided to turn from your life of selfishness and sin and let Jesus come into your life. At that moment of decision, you were given the power and privileges of a son or daughter. If God said it, He means it. Read it for yourself in this verse.

> But as many as received him, to them gave he power to become the sons of God, even to them that believe on his name.
>
> — John 1:12

You became a child of God, and the Father loves communicating with His children. Can you imagine a home where the parents never talked to the children? Unfortunately, this happens in too many homes today. The children say, "Yo, Dad. Hey, Mom," and the parents ignore them. Do you know what kind of family that is? Society calls it a dysfunctional family, and in too many instances the children of such a family are headed for the FBI's Most Wanted List.

How do we know this is true? The reason is the FBI cracked something sociologists and psychologists could not crack. They found some criminals come from wealthy families, some come from poverty, some are school dropouts and others are from the best of schools. But the FBI also discovered what the common thread is in criminal behavior, a dysfunctional, unconnected family.

As a Pastor, I know one common thread is that these people *chose* to be criminals. The other common thread the FBI found is simply that everyone on the FBI's Most Wanted List had no effective parental communication. They didn't feel loved by their parents because the parents didn't communicate love to them. Some of them were sent off to military schools and fancy private schools, but there was no bond between the parent and the child.

The Father Craves Your Fellowship

Communication is the common thread that binds a child with a parent. Now let me ask you this question, "Have *you* heard from the Lord lately?" The Father longs to communicate with you; He craves your fellowship. In fact, that was the whole reason why Jesus had to die. Sin in the Garden of Eden broke our fellowship with the Father. God loves us so much and wants to have communion and communication with us again and to be a family. That's why He sent Jesus, His only Son, to die on the cross, not for His sins, but for our sins. You can read in these verses just how much He loved us.

> For God so loved the world, that he gave his only begotten Son, that whosoever believeth in him should not perish, but have everlasting life. For God sent not his Son into the world to condemn the world, but that the world through him might be saved.
>
> — John 3:16,17 (KJV)

Whoever receives Jesus and believes that God raised Him from the dead becomes a child of God, and that opens up the line of communication again. Not only can we talk to God but also He speaks to us through His Word and His Spirit. Have you heard from the Lord lately?

If we are God's children, then what prevents us from hearing from the Lord? I want to discuss three specific reasons we limit our ability to hear God's voice.

Number One: We limit our ability to hear God's voice because we insist on a rational explanation for everything.

We try to figure everything out with our human, natural minds. We say, "Lord how is it that when I give, you multiply it back? I've got to figure this out before I can have the faith to give." Or perhaps we say, "Lord, how is it that a blind person can come to Mount Hope Church and walk away with his eyesight after the doctor said the condition is irreversible? I've got to figure this out before I'm going to believe it."

When God spoke to me about going into full-time ministry, it was clear and discernible; but I needed more evidence that it was God before I would step out in faith. I was happy where I worked. I had a great job that I loved, with benefits, insurance and friends there. Then God began to speak to me about going into full-time ministry with no guarantee of any income, no insurance, no pension and no benefits. It seemed like neon lights were flashing the words, "full-time ministry," in every magazine or book I picked up.

I thought it was God speaking but I was scared to make that step. I said, "Lord speak to me just one more time." I went to the bookstore to buy a book called *The Mark of the Beast.* I thumbed through the chapters and said, "Nothing about full-time ministry in there. It's all about prophecy." I paid for it and went home.

As I started reading the introduction, I discovered it was about how God called the author into the full-time ministry before he wrote this book! I said, "God, I know it's You speaking, but give me one more sign."

I drove up to the bank's drive-through teller window where my wife, Mary Jo, was working and said, "Mary Jo, I think God's telling us to go into full-time ministry."

She said, "Go resign and let's get started." I knew her confirmation was my sign. I resigned my job, and here I am today. My life is an adventure!

God's Ways Aren't Rational

How many have missed God's very best and most exciting and fascinating adventure for their lives because they had to figure it all out first? One cliché says, "If you can figure it out, it isn't God!" In other words, God works in ways that are not always rational or logical.

In his book, *Signs and Wonders Today*, Dr. C. Peter Wagner shares this story that defied the rationale of his theological beliefs at the time he was doing the research for his book:

> In 1965 Santa Rosa, Guatemala, in Central America was experiencing a terrible drought. People were leaving the city. Businesses were going bankrupt. Crops were perishing, and animals were dying. Special efforts were made to bring water into the city, but water was scarce every-

where. The Catholics were holding special masses. Evangelicals were holding prayer meetings. There was no rain and no water.

Then it happened. In a small Pentecostal meeting, where some believers were gathered for their regular worship service, the Spirit of the Lord moved in a mighty way. A message in tongues was given followed by an interpretation. It ran like this: 'Dig a well in the pastor's backyard. There you will find water.' There was much opposition from other churches as the deacons, elders and pastor began to dig. They thought these people were fanatics and/or were hallucinating — especially when they saw that the pastor's backyard was on a hill. A well would never be dug on a hill, as the water runs low. But the pastor, deacons and elders all continued to dig.

Soon one of the deacons became quite upset. 'Why is it in the pastor's backyard?' he asked. 'Why couldn't it be in mine?' Another elder thought perhaps the prophecy was biased. One deacon gave up. Another elder left. But there still remained a group ready to press on. Because of the drought the land was hard, so digging progressed slowly. On the fourth day they encountered a big boulder. It was so large they thought they had hit solid rock. But they kept digging around the boulder until finally, after two days, they were able to remove it. As they did so, a gush of water came forth. It was rich and plenteous, and they began to drink and drink.[2]

We all know this is the twenty first century and that kind of thing doesn't happen anymore, right? It may not seem rational. I'm telling you when you have a word from the Lord, it becomes a fascinating adventure. That well provided water for the whole city, and that church grew from 24 to 900 in one year. Why? Because something happened that the rational mind could not understand. God spoke and gave them a word! The city was saved because of a word given to a small group of people who believed God had spoken, and they didn't try to figure out why it couldn't be done. Have you heard from the Lord lately?

Number Two: We limit our ability to hear God's voice because we don't listen when He speaks.

When our children were younger, our family loved to take mini-vacations over to Grand Rapids, just an hour from our home. We had a favorite hotel with an indoor swimming pool, workout room, and free breakfast. Sometimes we went there just for an overnight "getaway." One big attraction was the hotel's parrot named Winslow that lived in the lobby. The kids loved to talk to Winslow.

There was a guy who bought a parrot and tried to get the parrot to talk. Now you all know that if you have a parrot, you want it to talk, unless you're a pirate or something and just want to carry it around on your shoulder for decoration. A parrot that doesn't talk is no fun at all.

The parrot's new owner said, "Polly want a cracker, Polly want a cracker," over and over and over. The parrot just stared back at him in silence. He bought long-play records and English grammar courses on tape and played them 24-hours a day, but that parrot still wouldn't talk.

He finally got fed up and said, "I'm taking you back to the store." The parrot still didn't talk. As he was walking across the road carrying the parrot to his car, another car was coming down the street toward them. The man didn't see it, but the parrot did and screeched, "Watch out, watch out." The guy said, "Oh shut up!" The car hit him but, fortunately, he was only bruised. He got up and brushed himself off mumbling something about that "dumb" parrot. The parrot said, "Me, dumb? You've been trying to teach me to talk for five years, and when I finally do, you don't listen to me."

Are You Tuned Into God's Channel?

How long has God been trying to talk to many of us but we aren't listening? Radio waves may be in a room, but you don't see them or hear them. Television signals are in your living room, but you don't see them going right through your body. When your television is hooked up to cable and tuned to the right channel and you turn it on, all of a sudden these waves that you can't see become visible images on the screen and audible sounds for you to hear what is being said.

Just as television and radio waves are always present, even though unseen, God too is speaking all the time. His thoughts toward you are too numerous to count. In other words, God has thoughts that are coming through like radio waves to speak to you.

One key to listening to God is getting on the right channel. The right channel requires that one first knows Jesus Christ as Lord and believes in what Jesus did on the cross at Calvary. An example of being on the right channel can be found in 1 Samuel, chapter 3. Samuel had never heard the voice of God, so he was not tuned in on the right channel. Once Eli instructed him how to listen and respond to God's voice, Samuel got on the right channel with the Lord and heard His voice clearly.

Eli was the high priest at the temple. Samuel was a little boy whose mother had dedicated him to the Lord and left him to live in the temple and be trained by Eli to serve God.

Samuel had gone to bed one night and heard a voice that said, "Samuel." Thinking it was Eli calling him, the boy got up and went to the priest saying, "Here I am; you called me."

"I didn't call you, go back to bed."

Samuel went back to bed, covered himself up, and heard the same voice again say, "Samuel." He had never heard God's voice before so, again, Samuel went in to the priest. Finally after the third time, Eli realized it must be the Lord. He instructed Samuel to go back to bed and if he heard the voice again, to say, "Speak, Lord, for your servant hears." Sure enough, it was God. God gave Samuel a word, and Samuel's life became a fascinating adventure. Are you listening when God speaks to you?

Number Three: We limit our ability to hear from God because we have preconceived notions of how He speaks.

Elijah had a preconceived notion of how God would speak to him. Elijah, by the way, was a cantankerous man. Yes, he was a prophet and had God's call, but his personality was like sandpaper. He was rough around the edges and rubbed everybody the wrong way. He just didn't like people. God bypassed his personality to use him the way God does with many people today.

When Elijah was running away from Jezebel, the wicked queen, he was hiding in a cave on the mountain of Horeb (the same mountain Moses spent time on years before). God came to him and said, "What are you doing here, Elijah?" (1 Kings 19:9).

Elijah was having his own pity party in that cave, and when God told him to stand before Him on the mountain, he remained in the cave hiding.

> Then He said, "Go out, and stand on the mountain before the LORD." And behold, the LORD passed by, and a great and strong wind tore into the mountains and broke the rocks in pieces before the LORD, but the LORD was not in the wind; and after the wind an earthquake, but the LORD was not in the earthquake; and after the earthquake a fire, but the LORD was not in the fire; and after the fire a still small voice. So it was, when Elijah heard it, that he wrapped his face in his mantle and went out and stood in the entrance of the cave. Suddenly a voice came to him, and said, "What are you doing here, Elijah?"
>
> — 1 Kings 19:11-13

Elijah expected to hear God's voice in the wind of a hurricane or in the shaking of an earthquake or in the flame of fire. He was surprised when after all of those monumental physical manifestations, God's voice came in a still small voice.

The word "still" in the Hebrew means, "a whispering." A whispering gentle voice within spoke to Elijah. This time he listened and knew it was God. We know that because he wrapped his mantel around his head and went out to stand before the

Lord at the mouth of the cave. He knew he had to protect his eyes from the glory of God. This time when God spoke, Elijah listened and obeyed.

You can study the life of Elijah after that experience and see that his whole personality was transformed. He wasn't the same old self that he was before he heard from God. His life became an exciting, fascinating adventure. In fact, he went to Heaven without ever dying. Now there's an adventure, isn't it?

God Speaks In Many Ways

Do you limit your ability to hear from God because you have to try to figure everything out or because you have preconceived notions of how He speaks or because you just don't listen? God speaks in so many different ways, and He loves to surprise us. He doesn't speak to everyone the same way so don't fall into the trap of comparing yourself with others. God is unique and loves variety.

The most important thing is taking time to listen, and that starts with being still. Have you ever tried to carry on a telephone conversation with someone who keeps talking so fast you can't get a word in? That's the way we are with God many times. We call Him on the prayer phone and then we don't stop talking long enough for Him to say anything. That is why

He says in Psalm 46:10, "Be still, and know that I am God."

The best way to hear from God is to get still when you first get up in the morning. How does your day begin? When the alarm goes off do you keep hitting the snooze button? When your feet finally hit the floor are you saying to yourself, "I don't know where I'm supposed to be, but I'm already an hour late?" If that is a picture of your morning, you are missing out on God's best for you. God has a word for you, and He speaks in the quiet of the morning to those who listen. As it says in His Word:

> The Lord GOD has given Me the tongue of the learned, that I should know how to speak a word in season to him who is weary. He awakens Me morning by morning, He awakens My ear to hear as the learned.
>
> — Isaiah 50:4

God will give you a word that will stick with you all day, a word that will "make your day," if you just give Him the chance. Have you heard from God lately? Who knows what fascinating adventure He has in store for you if you will allow Him to awaken your ears to hear Him each morning?

We have just begun to touch on how God speaks and the reasons why we don't hear Him. We live in the most exciting time in history. God is moving mightily on His people and awakening many who have been asleep for too long. The enemy has conspired against even the most learned to keep them from hearing God's voice, but his conspiracy has been uncovered as you will discover in the next chapter. God is still speaking to those who listen.

"How did we get so far from what Jesus said, to these doctrines that have robbed God's people of the power of the Holy Spirit?"

Chapter 2

The Great Conspiracy

Dr. Jack Deere, a professor at one of the most highly respected theological seminaries in the country, didn't believe miracles were for today or that God spoke to people today except by the written Scriptures. He was a scholar and a skeptic, which was why he took a group of Ph.D.'s with him to listen to a speaker who was causing quite a stir in the Christian community. Imagine Dr. Deere's shock when the guy sitting at the keyboard wearing a Hawaiian shirt and khaki pants was introduced as the speaker, John Wimber, the pastor of a 5,000-member church in Anaheim, California. He certainly didn't fit the image Dr. Deere and his associates had of a successful "reverend."

As John Wimber, pastor of the Anaheim Vineyard Church, opened his Bible and began to speak about the Kingdom of God, Dr. Deere was ready with pen and paper to note all of the inaccuracies this man would surely teach. After all, Dr. Deere's purpose in being there was to find fault and tear down whatever John Wimber might have to say about hearing God's voice and miracles.

Just then John Wimber stopped and said, "The Lord is showing me there is a lady here that has had a bad report from the doctor, and if you will come up here, God wants to heal you."

No one came forward and Dr. Deere sat there thinking, *"This guy is nuts."* He quickly made note of this foolishness in case he ever wanted to write a book about people who hear voices.

John Wimber wasn't fazed in the least as he continued, saying, "By the way, you went to the doctor on Tuesday at ten o'clock, and the doctor gave you a bad report from the tests you had. If you will come up here, God is going to heal you."

Still no one came forward. Dr. Deere was beginning to feel sorry for John Wimber thinking, *"This poor guy made this stuff up. Nobody is responding, and he is going to be so embarrassed."*

John Wimber calmly waited for a few minutes and then said, "The lady who went to the doctor at ten o'clock on Tuesday and was told you have an incurable disease; your name is Margaret. If you come up here, God will heal you."

A lady in the second row stood up crying and went forward. As John Wimber prayed for her, Dr. Deere was sitting there thinking, *"This is so cool."* Then another thought crossed his mind, *"What if he paid her to do that?"*

Suddenly, one of Dr. Deere's seminary colleagues stood up and said, "Oh my gosh, that's my sister-in-law, Margaret. She was diagnosed with cancer and told she didn't have long to live."[1]

Margaret was healed that night, and Jack Deere became a believer that people today can hear the voice of God. He went back to the seminary and began studying the Scriptures about hearing God's voice and miracles. He found out Jesus truly is *the same yesterday, today, and forever;* and that much of the theology he had been taught and was teaching others was flawed. Unfortunately, the seminary did not share in the excitement of Jack Deere's newfound truth and eventually released him from his position, but that hasn't stopped Jack Deere from sharing these truths in his book, *Surprised By The Voice Of God.*

The Supernatural Was The Norm

How did common practices in the early church fade into obscurity in the modern day church? In the Old and New Testaments, two-way communication between the Lord and various people, not just Jews or Christians, was recorded over and over again. God spoke to some audibly as well as in visions, dreams and trances. Angelic visitations were also accepted as the norm. People didn't seem surprised or frightened by these communications.

A good example is found in Acts chapter 10. Peter went up to the roof to pray and got hungry. He fell into a trance and saw a sheet descend from Heaven filled with all sorts of animals, wild beasts, birds and creeping things, which the Jews had been forbidden to eat. Let's read how this two-way conversation went.

> And a voice came to him, "Rise, Peter; kill and eat." But Peter said, "Not so, Lord! For I have never eaten anything common or unclean." And a voice *spoke* to him again the second time, "What God has cleansed you must not call common." This was done three times. And the object was taken up into heaven again.
>
> — Acts 10:13-16

When three messengers sent by Cornelius, a Roman centurion, arrived looking for Peter, he knew their arrival bore some significance to what he had seen in the trance. Then the Holy Spirit spoke to Peter and told him to go with these men. Look what the men told Peter about their boss.

> And they said, "Cornelius, *the* centurion, a just man, one who fears God and has a good reputation among all the nation of the Jews, was divinely instructed by a holy angel to summon you to his house, and to hear words from you."
>
> — Acts 10:22

Cornelius and his messengers were Gentiles and considered unclean by Jewish law, but he took instruction from an angel. Also, these soldiers didn't seem to find it out of the ordinary to make such a report to Peter.

Peter understood what God had said to him in the trance and obeyed these soldiers without question. It was a dramatic departure from Jewish law and tradition, but Peter took these men in and housed them and went with them to Cornelius' house. He preached the Gospel to Cornelius' household, and the Holy Spirit fell on those who *heard* the Word. These were probably the first Gentiles who were saved, filled with the Spirit, spoke in tongues and were baptized.

God Spoke And People Listened

In the days of the early church, when God spoke, people listened and obeyed. There was an intimacy between God's people and the Holy Spirit. Somehow, over the years, error crept into the religious teachings and the Holy Spirit was quenched. Today the Christian world has fallen prey to certain doctrines that have no biblical basis but are accepted and taught by theologians in Christian seminaries all over the world. We're going to discuss two such doctrines.

Cessation Doctrine

The first is the cessation doctrine, which says that after the full canon of the Scripture was written, the gifts of the Spirit ceased because, "that which is perfect is come." According to this doctrine there were only three periods of miracles — during the days of Moses, Elijah, Jesus and the Apostles. And once the entire Bible was written, there was no longer a need for miracles, visions, dreams or angelic intervention. In this doctrine there is not a need for God to speak to people because God's written Word is sufficient to meet all needs.

In explaining away the supernatural, such as the miracles we read about in Acts, there are four stages to the cessationist's argument:

1) *That's not normal.* Miracles are the exception not the norm.

2) *It was only for special people such as the apostles.* Interestingly enough, Stephen and

Philip, who performed miracles, cast out demons and operated fully in the gifts of the Spirit, were only deacons or lay people. Neither of them was an apostle, yet they heard God's voice and did mighty things in His name. Philip obeyed an angel and went out to the desert to meet an Ethiopian man. He had to run to catch up with the chariot, which was supernatural in and of itself. Philip preached the Gospel to him, got him saved and baptized, and then was caught away in an instant to another city. We call that "being transported in the Spirit."

3) *It was only for a special time or dispensation that God did these kinds of miracles.* This argument annihilates the Scripture in Hebrews 13:8 that says Jesus is the same yesterday, today and forever.

4) *This took place in the open canon, and you cannot use an illustration or take doctrine from the open canon.* The open canon is simply things that were written before the Bible was complete or before all of the Scriptures were canonized — officially accepted by the ecclesiastical Christian church as authentic and genuine. The point is how could the Bible be complete if it was still being written. Accord-

ing to this doctrine, every illustration or Scripture from the Bible becomes invalid because it was all written during the open canon.

The Deism Doctrine

Deism is the second doctrine of man that quenched the power of the Holy Spirit and the supernatural in the modern church. This doctrine further emphasizes that once the full canon of Scriptures was complete, there was no longer any need for the supernatural. The deists believe the Bible is God, and the only way God speaks is through the Bible. In effect, they worship the Bible. In other words, God created the world, wrote a book and then walked away saying, "Okay, you're on your own. I'll be back some day, but in the meantime if you get into trouble or have any questions, it's all in The Book."

I want you to know that God did *not* lose His voice because He wrote a book. I love the Bible and believe it is the inspired word of God. It *is* our instruction manual, and we need to look to it for revelation knowledge and wisdom. But the Bible didn't die on the cross for me. The Living Word of God, Jesus Christ, died on the cross for me. Jesus did not say, "When I go away, I will send you a book!" This is what He said:

> But now I go away to Him who sent Me, and none of you asks Me, 'Where are you going?'

> Nevertheless I tell you the truth. It is to your
> advantage that I go away; for if I do not go away,
> the Helper will not come to you; but if I depart, I
> will send Him to you. And when He has come,
> He will convict the world of sin, and of righ-
> teousness, and of judgment. However, when He,
> the Spirit of truth, has come, He will guide you
> into all truth; for He will not speak on His own
> *authority*, but whatever He hears He will speak;
> and He will tell you things to come.
>
> — John 16:5, 7-8, 13

So how did we get so far from what Jesus said, to these doctrines that have robbed God's people of the power of the Holy Spirit? There appears to have been a conspiracy to remove references to supernatural events in the historical writings of the Church.

What's Missing?

Men edited the writings of such great evangelists as Charles Spurgeon, Dwight Moody and Jonathan Edwards. Guess what has been edited out? The supernatural miracles and healings that took place at their meetings are missing. If you are able to find any of their original books, you will find references to many supernatural events. D.L. Moody describes the very day he was filled with the Holy Spirit and began to mumble unutterable words out of his mouth. He didn't call it tongues, but he declared how his altar calls quadrupled after this divine supernatural experience.

Charles Spurgeon wrote of quaking and shakings in churches. Jonathan Edwards wrote of people falling out under the power in his meetings. Sixteenth century writings tell of preachers in Scotland and England laying hands on the sick to heal them. The writings of Martin Luther refer to his speaking in tongues and commanding his servant, Marconius, in the name of Jesus to rise up and be healed. Frederick Marconius rose up from his deathbed and outlived Martin Luther.

Many modern writings have been watered down to support the more accepted teachings of today.

George Wishart was regarded as a prophet in his day. *Scots Worthies*, a biography of Wishart's life written by John Howie in 1775 said, "He possessed the spirit of prophecy in an extraordinary degree." In 1846 this same book was edited and expanded and this statement was revised to read, "He possessed an extraordinary degree of sagacious foresight."[2] This revision inferred that Wishart was able to accurately *guess* at how events would turn out because of his own wisdom, not God's.

The editor of the 1846 edition justified this change by saying that the Scottish Reformers made a mistake regarding the nature of prophecy because prophecy is no longer given. This editor felt fully justified to revise the text to fit his own theology. A prophecy Wishart gave before his execution came about exactly as prophesied three months after Wishart's death. The prophecy was watered down and explained away as simple coincidence by this same editor.[3]

Such editing became commonplace as old manuscripts were published in later years. Man's doctrine replaced God's truth, and error crept into the Church.

Modern Day Acts

The story you read at the beginning of this chapter about Jack Deere, a highly educated professor being deceived into believing and even teaching doctrines of man that deny God speaks today or that supernatural miracles happen in our times, is not unique.

Dr. C. Peter Wagner, professor of Church Growth at Fuller Theological Seminary in California, visited Argentina to study the explosion of church growth that was happening there. What he saw shook his theology to the roots. He discovered that miracles, dreams, visions, and hearing God's voice *are* for today, just like it was in the book of Acts. Dr. Wagner has since written a three-book commentary titled, *The Acts of the Holy Spirit Series*. He says this about Christianity today:

"Many modern Christians are not satisfied with Christianity as usual. They are fed up with playing church. The status quo has little appeal. Their desire is to look at the end of the day or at the end of the year and say, 'Praise God! His Kingdom has advanced and He has allowed me to be a part of it.' They don't want to be spectators, they want to be participants in the great work God is doing today... Acts was designed to be God's training manual for modern Christians. Seeing what worked so well almost 2,000 years ago will directly apply to our service to God today and can provide a welcome power boost to the Christian life."[4]

There are still many scholars and theologians today who are denying God's voice and His power. I recently read an article titled, "Does God Do Miracles Today?" It was written by the president of a well-known Bible institute that trains thousands of preachers who are in the pulpits around America. The whole thesis of the article was poking fun at the supernatural because God does not need to do miracles today.

But for all those who are still caught up in such doctrine, God is lighting a fire of truth in hundreds of others like Dr. Jack Deere and Dr. C. Peter Wagner who are speaking and writing the truth that the Bible didn't do away with or replace the supernatural, and that God still speaks to us today through the voice of the Holy Spirit and in dreams, visions, angels and supernatural gifts. God is using many highly educated and respected people to validate the move of His Spirit for this generation.

I want to make it very clear that I am not standing in judgment of those who may disagree with what I see happening in the supernatural realm. God's timing is perfect. He has allowed certain things to remain hidden for such a time as this. I pray that those who still don't have ears to hear will be enlightened to the truth.

The River Is Rising

The power of the Holy Spirit being experienced through the body of Christ today has grown in stages according to His purpose. The flow began with a trickle in the early days of the twentieth century in the Azusa Street revivals. It became a stream in the late 40s, pouring into a broader flow beginning in the 60s and 70s, until in the last ten years we have seen the river rising.

The conspiracy has been uncovered and it's time to change whatever attitudes and beliefs have hindered you from having ears to hear. I invite you to get in the river. You may be wading in shallow water but it is time to go out deeper. Don't let the river pass you by because of fear or lack of knowledge. Keep reading and you will discover what the Bible *does* and what it *doesn't do.*

"We live in a violent, unstable world, and it is critical that we hear the omniscient voice of God."

Chapter 3

What The Bible Doesn't Do!

Upon leaving his position with the theological seminary, Dr. Jack Deere felt he needed to learn more about how to operate in the power of the Holy Spirit. He moved to California and joined John Wimber as an associate at Anaheim Vineyard Church.

One Sunday Dr. Deere decided to visit the ten- to twelve-year-old children's church. He didn't pray or give it too much forethought or preparation. After all, he knew the Bible inside and out. What could a group of children this age ask that he couldn't answer? However, God's lesson that day was more for Dr. Deere than it was for the children in that children's church.

Dr. Deere said to the children, "I'm here to answer any questions you might have. What would you like to ask me?"

One young boy said, "Dr. Deere, why do bad things happen to good people?"

"Well, God doesn't want us to be robots but rather friends with freedom and dignity."

These kids kept asking tough questions and they weren't satisfied with pat answers. This question and answer routine went on for forty-five minutes, and Dr. Deere didn't have all the answers for them. By that time he was really irritated and said, "Okay, that's enough. I'm not taking any more questions. Kids you can ask him," pointing to the prophetically gifted pastor who had accompanied Dr. Deere. This young man loved the Bible, but he had also prayed and asked the Lord to show him what the Spirit of God was saying for these children. Dr. Deere looked at him in desperation and said, "Do you have anything to say to them?"

"Yes, as a matter of fact I do. This little girl over here with the red hair and freckles, what's your name?"

"J-J-Julie."

"Julie, God showed me you were in your bedroom last Tuesday night crying really hard. You were saying over and over, 'God, do you really love me? God, do you really love me?' You didn't hear God say anything then, but He told me to come and tell you that He really does love you, and all the trouble that is going on in your life is not your fault." Julie just cried and cried. This young man went on and spoke to several other children that day.[1]

Afterward, Dr. Deere went to Julie and said, "Julie, last Tuesday night were you in your bedroom crying really hard, and did you ask God if He really loved you?"

"Yes."

"Are your parents fighting now?"

"Yes."

"Are they talking about getting a divorce?"

"Yes."

"Do you think that's your fault?"

She looked up at him, smiled and said, "Not any more."[2]

Dr. Deere repented before the Lord for not even praying before he went to those children. He had plenty of Bible knowledge but that wasn't what God wanted to give to those children that day. The young man had inquired of the Spirit how to minister to the children and was given the words to speak encouragement to a brokenhearted little girl and others.

The Bible is a book written by the inspired word of God, but Jesus is the *Living* Word. The Bible was not given to replace the Holy Spirit, and the Holy Spirit did not come to replace the Bible. The Bible was not given to replace the supernatural, and supernatural was not given to replace the Bible. The Bible was not given to replace spiritual gifts, and spiritual gifts were not given to replace the Bible. Each has its purpose.

The Bible can tell us that the Holy Spirit is a comforter. But only the Holy Spirit can tell us that little Julie is struggling and needs a special word from God. If we are listening to His voice, He sometimes speaks at the most unexpected moments, as you'll read in this next story.

A Divine Appointment

A minister was driving through Florida and saw a sign that said, "Fresh Squeezed Orange Juice, Next Right." His wife noticed it as well and said, "Let's pull off and get some orange juice." They turned onto the side road and traveled quite a distance before coming to another sign directing them to turn right. When they reached the orange grove, a woman came running out to their car and said, "Are you a minister?"

"Yes, how did you know?"

"I've been so sick and have been praying God would send somebody to lay hands on me and pray. The Lord said, 'I'm sending someone, and you'll know them because they'll be driving a station wagon and pulling a trailer.' Now here you are!"

This minister and his wife thought they were going to get some fresh orange juice, but God had set up a divine appointment for them. Don't you just love it when God speaks? Supernatural gifts have not ceased and miracles do still happen.[3]

"Jesus, You Heard Me!"

One night in a Bible study we were worshipping the Lord, and I had a vision of a sixteen-year-old young man crying out to God in the wee hours of the morning about a particular problem. I didn't know quite how to address this so I just closed my eyes and said; "The Lord said He saw you in your bedroom in the wee hours of the morning crying out to him." Suddenly a young man in the group shot up in the air, his feet came right out from under him and he fell flat on his back screaming and crying, "That was me! That was me! Thank you, Jesus. You heard me!"

Everything Is Okay!

Another time a lady from our church called me at seven o'clock at night and said, "I'm worried. My daughter is driving up from Dallas. She said she would be here by six o'clock, and she has never been late before. I'm afraid something happened on the highway."

I quietly asked the Lord to give me a word for this woman. I said, "Everything is okay. You're going to hear from her by eleven o'clock tonight. Don't worry."

At 11:15 p.m. my phone rang. It was the mother, and she said, "My daughter's okay. She's safe. She got in a traffic jam in Kansas and stopped to get a bite to eat. She called at 10:45 p.m. and said she would be home by midnight."

We serve a living God. He still speaks to us today if we train our ears to hear and take the time to be still and listen. Sometimes God will speak through one of us to give prophetic warning like He did for Mordecai Ham, a Baptist evangelist in the early 1900s.

A Prophet's Warning

As Dr. Ham was preaching in Charlotte, North Carolina, two young women were heckling and harassing him by making smart remarks every time he said something. They created quite a disturbance. He stopped and said, "Please stop that, you're grieving the Holy Spirit." Another time he said to them,

"Please stop that. The Holy Spirit is speaking to people's hearts and this is important." He addressed them numerous times, but each time they would heckle and make even more harassing remarks. Finally after forty-five minutes or so of long suffering, Dr. Ham stopped his sermon and said, "Ladies, I'm sorry I have to announce to you that neither one of you will see the sun rise tomorrow."

Instead of being disturbed by such a warning, they got up in a huff and went home. Dr. Ham continued on with his meeting.

The next morning people who had been in the meeting were shocked to learn there had been a fire in the apartment building where these two young women lived. Everyone escaped unharmed except the two women who had received the prophecy from Dr. Ham. They lived on opposite ends of the building but both perished in the fire.[4]

God didn't give us the Bible to replace the prophets, and He didn't give us prophets to replace the Bible. We live in a violent, unstable world, and it is critical that we hear the omniscient voice of God. The Bible instructs us to go into all the world and preach the Gospel, but only the Holy Spirit can warn us of danger and tell us when and where we are <u>not</u> to go. That is why we must have ears to hear His voice.

"We must hear God's voice and walk under the covering and protection of God in these unstable times. It may be a matter of life and death."

Chapter 4

Why *Must* We Have Ears To Hear?

I'm not one of those people who constantly says God told me this or that. I won't say it unless I *know* God told me. Such is the case with a dramatic vision I had in 1985. It was a Thursday morning at 9:07 a.m. in the prayer chapel. I saw an ugly stick that looked like it had warts on it and was covered with rust, scum and mold. This ugly stick was going through a hollow tube and inside that tube was a great fire and a whirlwind. When I saw the stick come out the other end of the hollow tube, it was a golden shaft of the purest gold I have ever seen. It was almost transparent.

I said, "Lord, I couldn't have thought that up myself. I don't think about grubby, ugly sticks. What are you trying to say to me or show me?"

He said, "That stick you saw is My Church. I'm coming for a Church that is holy, without spot, without wrinkle and without blemish."

I knew He was speaking to me corporately and individually. I got the sense that I also looked like that ugly stick going through the fire.

He said, "Because My people have not judged themselves, they must be judged."

Tested By Fire

I was so shook as God began to unfold the revelation of this vision I had to leave the chapel and return to my office. You may have read about the fire that declares whether your works are wood, hay or stubble in the following Scripture:

> For no other foundation can anyone lay than that which is laid, which is Jesus Christ. Now if anyone builds on this foundation *with* gold, silver, precious stones, wood, hay, straw, each one's work will become clear; for the Day will declare it, because it will be revealed by fire; and the fire will test each one's work, of what sort it is.
>
> — 1 Corinthians 3:11-13

That fire is coming. We have often read of this as the judgment seat of Christ. However, because we have not judged ourselves, there will be judgment *before* Christ returns. It is the only way the Church, which is the Bride of Christ, will be spotless and without blemish. When we come through the fire of this judgment, we will be as pure as the purest gold. Remember, it is easier to judge ourselves than to have God do it.

It has been fifteen years since I had that vision. We have seen some judgment in the Church but we still have a long way to go. The fire has not yet been hot enough, and we have been too quick to judge others without looking at the ugliness of our own stick. A good example is what took place in the White House in 1999.

Accuser Or Intercessor?

At a prophetic conference in Colorado Springs in early 1999, the word of the Lord came forth from God's prophets. In summary, this is what they said, "God is more disappointed in His Church than He is disappointed in the President because, by and large, the Church took up Satan's role of accuser instead of Jesus' role of intercessor. God has called the Church to pray for those in authority, but the Church spent its time accusing, ridiculing and developing bumper stickers . . .."

God puts those in authority over nations and it's our role to intercede and pray for them. We haven't gotten there yet and judgment is coming. Did you know some studies have shown an alarmingly high percentage of Christian men are hooked on pornography? If your personal life were scrutinized as closely as President Clinton's was, how would you fare?

In a recent newspaper column a woman wrote that after her father died, she was cleaning out his closets and found a collection of child pornography, which had come from the Internet. She was shocked and horrified to discover her loving, "decent" father had been involved in this filth. She burned the material in the fireplace as she prayed for each of the young girls involved.

The news columnist shared the woman's letter with a psychologist, one of the nation's top authorities on sexual compulsions and addiction. The psychologist said, "The Internet is probably the biggest crisis in my field. It is the crack cocaine of sexual addiction. And because of the Internet's availability and anonymity, more and more of them are women."[1]

A Window Of Opportunity

I won't go into the specifics of the prophecies given at that prophetic conference in January of 1999, but they were sobering. Many who hear such words shrug them off as just "doom and gloom." Isn't that what the people of Israel did to the prophets of old? We must accept the critical role of prophecy in present times and listen to the voice of the prophets in our day. Judgment is coming. We only have a small window of opportunity to stop it by doing two things.

Number one is to repent. If you have ever stood in the role of accuser instead of the role of an intercessor, you need to repent. If there is lawlessness in your heart today, you need to repent. If you have never made Jesus Lord of your life, now is the time to repent.

Number two is to intercede. We must pray for our leaders, cities, and our nation. You may be able to create a pocket of safety in your community. The Lord showed me this one morning in prayer. He said, "Dave, in whatever city I have a praying church that is repenting and interceding, I will protect that area from the worst of what is to come." Take advantage of this opportunity to impact your city and nation. Don't quit or slack off because nothing seems to be happening. Those that endure to the end are going to see victory.

Hear And Obey

We *must* hear God's voice and walk under the covering and protection of God in these unstable times. It may be a matter of life and death. One young man from Columbine High School was interviewed by CNN news after the shootings in April 1999. The interviewer asked him how he escaped, and he said,

"I was hiding and praying to the Lord for understanding and help on what to do. I heard a voice that said, 'Get out now.' I simply obeyed that voice because I knew it was God speaking to me. I crawled out from my hiding place and walked right out to safety. It was as if God made me invisible."

Another young woman at Columbine School was asked the same question in a news interview, and her response was almost identical. She said she was praying to Jesus and He made her invisible. She was able to walk right by the shooters without being harmed.

Nowhere To Run

National statistics have tried to convince us there has been a decrease in crime rates over the past seven years. However, as one news reporter wrote after the September 1999 shootings at Wedgwood Baptist Church in Ft. Worth, Texas, "The headlines bleed through the statistics . . . but month after month, even week after week, the nation has been assaulted by horrific stories of innocents attacked or slain."

He went on to report that the reason is because in the past killers were usually someone close to the victim or someone the victim shouldn't have been close to, such as a drug dealer or gang member. But the attacks we are seeing in schools and even in churches are different in that the innocent victims have been in what should have been the right place, a safe place.[2]

Wedgwood Baptist Church was hosting a special concert for high school students in the Dallas/Ft. Worth Metroplex, who had participated in, "See You at the Pole Day," a student-led prayer day held annually at schools across the country. The church sanctuary was filled with teens from a number of schools and churches when a gunman walked in and began shooting, killing seven and critically wounding seven more before turning the gun on himself.

Such violence is taking place in the workplace, in schools, and now even in churches. From January through August 1999 there were ten such shootings. We must pray continually on a daily and even hourly basis to seek God's wisdom and protection. Being at the wrong place at the wrong time can be deadly. We need God's guidance.

A Threat To The Enemy

Our children and young people are under attack. This was prophesied at the January 1999 prophetic conference in Colorado Springs I spoke of earlier. In an article published after the Wedgwood shootings, several religious leaders confirmed this as well. The Dallas-area organizers for "See You at the Pole" said,

"The recent assaults are nothing less than the front line of a faith-based assault." The director of a Youth Outreach Network in Irving, Texas said, "We believe there is a spiritual war going on. Without sounding too crazy, Satan has escalated the battle from the spiritual to the physical. These Christian kids represent a threat to him." The FBI chaplain in Oklahoma City who helped coordinate counseling for the survivors of the bombing said, "There's a war for the hearts of young people. For the past year, I've been making presentations around the country and predicting these things are going to happen in public places, including churches."[3]

A Call To Prayer

My purpose in discussing these events and prophecies is not to scare you but rather to call you to prayer and emphasize the critical need to have ears to hear what God is saying in these times.

Chuck Pierce, the director of the World Prayer Center in Colorado Springs, preached a message at a church in Dallas in November 1999 just a short time after the bonfire tragedy at Texas A & M that killed and injured a number of students. In his message Chuck shared two very significant things that came out of a time of intercessory prayer while he was in College Station, Texas on April 19, 1999 for a meeting with community and church leaders. Texas A & M is located in College Station. He was only there for one day, but while he was there a spirit of intercession came on him strongly. He lay down on the floor in his hotel room and began to pray and intercede.

The first thing that happened was the Lord showed him something tragic would happen at Texas A & M before the end of the year that would bring them into national attention. However, the Lord was going to use the circumstances greatly to work His purposes out in that area, especially in the body of Christ to unite, renew, and awaken them in a new way and propel forward a "revival anointing" in the students. As Chuck later shared this with community and church leaders, he said, "Let's all agree out of this tragedy that will happen."

Testimony Of Grace

After the bonfire collapsed in early November 1999, the leaders remembered this word Chuck had shared with them, and it encouraged them to unite and move together in a new way. If any of you saw the TV news coverage or read any of the accounts, a number of the students who were killed were strong Christians. Many students were seen praying together and spoke openly of the faith of their friends and their own faith in the midst of this tragedy. It was an awesome testimony of God's loving grace.

The second thing that happened to Chuck during his time of intercession in April was feeling a sense of panic that something was terribly wrong at his children's school in Colorado Springs. He prayed and couldn't get past it. He called his wife but no one was at home. Then he called his office, and when he asked to talk with his assistant, a temporary receptionist said, "Oh, you can't. He just ran out the door to go to your house." Chuck was in such a state he called his brother who said, "Chuck, nothing is wrong, get a grip."

The next day, as Chuck arrived home in Colorado Springs, news of the Columbine School shootings was being broadcast across the nation. Chuck's family was safe, but tragedy had struck in the not-so-distant Colorado community of Columbine. The Lord said to Chuck, "My people have got to come to a place where they will *press in, wait* for me and *listen* for me so they can hear very, very accurately *all* of what I am saying. If they will do that, I will give them the authority to overthrow lawlessness that is working in this land."[4]

Rejoice In His Goodness

We have discussed the need to become repenters and intercessors, but we must also become rejoicers. Rachel Scott was one of the students killed in the Columbine School shootings. She had been a sold-out, radically saved Christian for over four years when she died. In death she reached millions of people as CNN broadcast her funeral around the world. The service was a celebration of God's goodness and love. The Gospel was presented in drama, in personal testimonies and in songs of praise by family and friends. A message centered on Jesus Christ was preached by the pastor.

It was said that over 150 people came forward to accept the Lord at the end of the service. Only God knows how many lives were touched and changed as people worldwide viewed this service on TV. Death was swallowed up in victory that day. The enemy is absolutely defeated when we rejoice in circumstances he would try to use to destroy us. There is no greater weapon than rejoicing in the goodness of God when circumstances appear to be evil.

Time is short and the countdown has begun. Judgment will come. It is almost irreversible now, but God would rather exercise mercy than judgment. We have a small window of opportunity to repent and intercede for God to temper His judgment with mercy.

What are you doing to keep this window open? Are you praying for your church, community and nation? Are you pressing in, waiting and listening to hear God's voice? Don't waste another moment, hour or day. This is the hour to have ears to hear. Have you heard from the Lord lately?

Hearing God's voice doesn't just come automatically. That is why we are going to explore God's guidance-on-the-go system that provides practical ways to hear God's voice and apply His truth in our daily lives.

Chapter 5

Guidance-On-The-Go

Shock gripped the nation that Saturday morning of July 17, 1999 as news spread of the disappearance off the coast of Martha's Vineyard of the privately owned plane piloted by John F. Kennedy Jr., that also carried his wife, Carolyn, and his sister-in-law, Lauren Bessette. As hours turned into days, the search continued for possible survivors, and later for the wreckage and bodies of victims of yet another Kennedy tragedy.

Although the exact cause of the crash may never be known, experts believe it was due to spacial disorientation caused by a pilot untrained in flying with instruments. They believe he became disoriented by poor visibility on a moonless night off the Massachusetts coast. Other pilots said it must have been like flying into a black hole.

The 1995 single-engine Piper Saratoga that Kennedy had owned for only a few months was equipped with the finest equipment. It included an automatic pilot and a satellite-guided global positioning system, which would have drawn a straight line from Essex County airport to Martha's Vineyard regardless of the weather. Unfortunately, Kennedy was not an instrument-rated pilot. Therefore he was relying on his visual senses to keep the plane level and on course.

Veteran pilots know that without being able to fly by instruments, it only takes two or three minutes to lose sight of the horizon and become disoriented. A plane can actually flip upside down in the blink of an eye, and the pilot cannot tell which way is up or down. Once a pilot's senses are confused, it is difficult to maintain control of the plane and it may easily plunge into a sudden dive.

Experts believe this is what happened to Kennedy. The FAA's air-traffic radar showed his plane cruising at 5,500 feet for about an hour and then going into a steep dive, disappearing from radar at 1,300 feet.[1] He was a licensed pilot with a fully-equipped plane, but because he didn't know how to use the instruments and guidance system, he lost control of the plane and crashed.

This is so similar to what happens to many Christians. They accept Jesus into their hearts and join God's air force with all the excitement and daring of a new pilot. They have the Bible as their training manual, but they are inexperienced in applying His principles to everyday life. When they get into trouble, they try to use the Bible to guide them and their visual senses to get them out of it. They don't realize the risk they are taking, and without the Holy Spirit's guidance, they often lose their way and crash. That is why we need the written word of the Bible <u>and</u> the guidance of the Holy Spirit in our lives.

As a licensed pilot, I have two books that are absolutely necessary. One is called the FAR, the Federal Aviation Regulations, and the other is called the AIM, which is the Airman's Instruction Manual. These manuals are published together annually and are what pilots refer to as the FAR/AIM. They provide the flying industry's foundational regulations and instructions for flying an aircraft. It's all in there.

However, airplanes are also equipped with instruments and navigational equipment. We have the Loran guidance system and global positioning systems that run off satellites. We have Vortac (V.O.R.) navigational aides, radios, ILS approach equipment, VASSI and PAPI landing guidance systems, and a number of other things to guide us in flight, to help us get to our destination, and to land safely. As I am flying, I watch the needle on the Loran. If the needle goes a little to the right, I know I've got to turn the plane a little to the right to stay on course. That is how pilots are guided en route. I call this guidance-on-the-go.

Imagine a pilot saying this to you: "Come fly with me. I don't understand any of this navigational equipment. I don't even use it. As long as I have the FAR/AIM and my pilot's license, that's all I need. I don't need any guidance. I just get in the airplane and go." Would you want to fly with that pilot?

Believe it or not, John F. Kennedy Jr. made a similar statement in an interview with *USA Today* in May 1998. He had gotten his pilot's license only a few weeks before, but none of his relatives could be persuaded to fly with him. He said, "The only person I've been able to get to go up with me, who looks forward to it as much as I do, is my wife. The second it was legal, she came up with me. Now, whenever we want to get away, we can just get in a plane and fly off."[2]

I'm not implicating that someone who isn't an instrumented-rated pilot should never fly, but such a pilot should use wisdom and consider the risks of quickly changing weather and other factors. Night flying and flying over water are especially hazardous. In such circumstances, the FAR/AIM is not enough nor can a pilot simply rely on his or her visual senses. The point I am making here is that any pilot who says all he or she needs is the FAR/AIM is as foolish as Christians saying all they need is the Bible.

We need the written word in the Bible as our foundation, but we also need the Holy Spirit to guide us every single day of our lives. In the next three chapters I am going to share with you three keys to developing God's guidance-on-the-go system in your life. The first is building the proper foundation on God's Word. The second is waiting on God for direction, and the third is following the Holy Spirit's guidance. These are fundamental principles you need to live successfully in God's kingdom here on earth.

"God's Word never changes. It is established forever to lead, guide and teach us."

Chapter 6

Key Number 1: Building The Proper Foundation On God's Word

In 1372 an unusual and very unique new building was dedicated in Italy. This twelve-story, solid marble structure began to sink before it was even dedicated, but the builders went ahead and finished it any way. Today it is approximately twelve feet out of plum and leans rather precariously. If you haven't already guessed, this building is known as the "Leaning Tower of Pisa," a popular tourist attraction.

The Tower is sinking at about one-quarter inch per year because it was built on marshland, and the foundation is only ten feet deep, which is not adequate for a twelve-story, solid marble structure. If something is not done soon, by the year 2007 the building will have leaned too far, and engineering experts predict it will collapse.

In contrast, you can go to other cities in England and Europe and visit numerous old cathedrals that were built in the 1300's and 1400's. They are still standing perfectly solid and straight with nothing out of line. These cathedrals were built with foundations beneath them that go down deeper than the height of the structure you see visibly reaching to the sky. It is the foundation that makes the difference.

As Christians we need a solid foundation in God's written word, the Bible. Just as the Federal Aviation Regulations and the Airmen's Instruction Manual, known as the FAR/AIM, is every pilot's foundation, the Bible must be every Christian's foundation. The only difference is that when we read, study, and meditate on the words in the Bible, they are alive and powerful. These are not the words of mere men but rather words inspired by the Holy Spirit for directing and guiding our lives, as we can read in Hebrews.

> For the word of God *is* living and powerful, and sharper than any two-edged sword, piercing even to the division of soul and spirit, and of joints and marrow, and is a discerner of the thoughts and intents of the heart.
>
> — Hebrews 4:12

Learn His Language

The Bible, or the Word of God, is written in the language of the Holy Spirit. We must become students of the Word in order to learn His vocabulary, which blends the Spirit and the Truth. Jesus is the Truth and He said:

> **The Spirit gives life; the flesh counts for nothing. The words I have spoken to you are spirit and they are life.**
>
> **— John 6:63 (NIV)**

The Word of God gives you the ability to distinguish the difference between what is spiritual and what is just mere emotion. Sometimes people go to a church service or an evangelistic meeting and their emotions get so stirred up and excited, they think it is the Spirit of God. Then they may make some foolish decisions based on their emotions because they cannot discern what is really the Spirit of God. The reason this happens is because they don't have a solid foundation in the Word of God. They don't know the language and vocabulary of the Spirit, so they are easily deceived by what tickles their emotions and makes them feel good.

We can read about an example of people being stirred by their emotions versus those who search out wisdom in the Scriptures. The apostle Paul, along with Silas and Timothy, was preaching the Gospel in Thessalonica when some of the Jews began stirring up people's emotions and actually incited a riot, blaming it on Paul's teachings. The Christians had to send Paul and Silas away to protect them. Then they arrived in the city of Berea and began teaching in the synagogue there. Read how differently the Berean's responded.

> These were more fair-minded than those in Thessalonica, in that they received the word with all readiness, and *searched the Scriptures daily to find out* whether these things were so. Therefore many of them believed, and also not a few of the Greeks, prominent women as well as men.
>
> — Acts 17:11,12

Building a Christian life based on God's guidance-on-the-go system begins with developing a foundation in God's written Word. God's Word never changes. It is established forever to lead, guide and teach us, as it says here:

> Forever, O LORD, Your word is settled in heaven.
>
> — Psalm 119:89

Set Your Daily Priorities

Reading, studying and meditating on God's Word should be a high priority every day. As we just read, the Berean's found their way to Jesus by reading and studying the Scriptures on a daily basis. They weren't caught up in any emotional upheaval like the Thessalonian's; they examined the Scripture and found the truth for themselves instead of listening to what other men told them. No matter what other people say to me, I am sticking with the foundation of God's Word in the Bible. It is just as up-to-the-minute today as it was when it was written.

Let me give you an interesting illustration about setting priorities. Suppose I have a wide-mouthed, gallon mason jar, and I fill it with as many large rocks as I can fit in it. Would you say it is full? You'd say, "Yes, it's full. You can't fit any more rocks in it."

Then I pour gravel into the jar and the gravel filters down between all the crevices around the rocks and I ask, "Okay, now is it full?" Your answer would be, "Yes, it is definitely full now."

But I'm not finished with this experiment. Next I take some fine sand and pour it in so that it filters down between the tiny cracks and crevices not filled by the gravel and rocks. What is your answer this time? I'm sure you would say, "Oh, yes. It's full. You can't get anything else in that jar."

But I have one more step. I pour water into the jar until it spills over the brim.

It is full. What would have happened if I had reversed the order of the things I put in the jar? It wouldn't have worked. If I put the water and sand in first, there wouldn't have been room for any gravel and definitely not the larger rocks.

The jar in this illustration represents your time each day, and the rocks represent the foundation of God's Word. If you don't put the large rocks in first thing in the day, there probably won't be room for them later in the day. That's why the first thing every morning, I open God's Word in my gallon jug of time because His Word is the biggest Rock in my life. If you know anything about effective time management, you know that you must prioritize your time doing the most important things first. Otherwise, your time will be filled with little inconsequential things that won't really help develop your guidance-on-the-go system.

The right foundation for an effective guidance-on-the-go system begins with reading, studying, meditating on, hearing and knowing God's voice through His Holy Word, the Bible. When you have such a solid foundation inside of you, there will be no question whose voice you are hearing because you will recognize His language and vocabulary.

Recently a news article reported an incident in a middle school in Germantown, Maryland. Six students had accused a male gym teacher of sexual mis-conduct. This teacher was well respected and had an impeccable reputation, but the school was forced to suspend him while an investigation was conducted. The students claimed the gym teacher had gone into the girls' locker room and inappropriately touched several girls while they were in their underwear and even called one of them "a hot sexy mama."

As the police questioned the students who made the accusations, the police had doubts about their stories. Each time they were questioned the stories expanded in detail and didn't line up with any other witnesses. One of the key investigators expressed his doubt saying, "'Hot sexy mama' is just not language used by people in our generation. That's kid's stuff."[1]

In interviewing one of the girls the investigator said, "This is serious business, and it's going to have some serious consequences. If it didn't happen, tell me now. Let's end it."[2]

The girl began to cry and admitted it had never happened. Subsequently all of the students recanted their stories. A teacher's reputation was saved be-cause, among other things, an investigator recognized that the language or vocabulary used in the accusa-tion didn't line up with what a man the teacher's age would normally use.

It is important to know God's language so you won't be deceived. The Bible will always confirm what the Spirit is saying to you. If what you are hearing contradicts or doesn't line up with God's Word, you can be sure it isn't God's voice you are hearing.

Wait For His Direction

The second key to God's guidance-on-the-go system is waiting on God for His direction. Most of us don't like waiting. Our "microwave" society wants instant service and instant gratification. We are constantly looking for faster routes to get places, faster cars, fast food and definitely faster computers. "Road rage" has increased on our highways because some drivers get incensed by having to wait in traffic.

One such incident made national news. A man, who was angry because traffic was tied up in his lane, jumped out of his car, ran to the car ahead of him, snatched the woman's little white dog out of her lap and killed the dog by throwing it into oncoming traffic. He got back in his car and drove off to the horror of the dog's owner and others who witnessed it.

Jesus' last commandment to His disciples was to wait. He had gone to the cross, rose from the dead and spent several days with them. As He was getting ready to go back to Heaven, He said:

Behold, I send the Promise of My Father upon you; but tarry in the city of Jerusalem until you are endued with power from on high.

— Luke 24:49

He didn't tell them how long they were going to have to wait. As it turned out, it was ten days. Those who waited received the promise, being filled with the power of the Holy Spirit at Pentecost. They returned to Jerusalem preaching and teaching the Gospel of Jesus and turned the world upside down for God. We must wait on the Holy Spirit so He can lead, teach and guide us, as we will learn in the next chapter.

"In God's presence your heart will develop sensitivity to His guidance system."

Chapter 7

Key Number 2: Waiting On God For Direction

A lady was walking through a park one day carrying her Polaroid camera. Two kids ran by, grabbed her camera and ran off. She screamed and a policeman on foot patrol was there in less than a minute. She told him what had just happened and he took off after them in the direction she had seen them run.

As the two kids ran off, they realized the camera was a Polaroid that took pictures and developed them instantly. They took a picture of each other. Each time, the camera buzzed and spit out a white piece of shiny paper. The boys glanced at the white paper and said, "This thing doesn't work." They threw the papers on the ground and kept going taking more pictures and throwing the white paper on the ground each time as they went.

For the policeman this was better than a trail of breadcrumbs in the Hansel and Gretel story. He picked up the pictures and knew he wasn't far behind them because the pictures were in the final developing stage. He found a picture of one thief and then a picture of the other one. Pretty soon, he caught up with the two thieves and collared them. They denied taking the camera until he showed them their pictures. The lady got her camera back and the two kids got juvenile hall. They didn't know they had to *wait* for the picture to develop.

Don't Quit Too Soon!

We don't like to wait. We pray for something and think God should answer instantaneously. If we pray for a car, we think we should walk out the door and find it sitting in the driveway. Then we give up and let go of our faith too quickly. I have learned that God's ways are not my ways, and His timing is definitely not according to my watch. In reality, the greatest thing we can do is to wait on the Lord. The eleven disciples learned that from Jesus and their reward was great.

Humble Yourself And Wait

It takes humility to wait before the Lord, because pride wants to swing into action and *do* something. Most often that means we are going to do it our way and not God's way. Over the years I have learned to wait on the Lord before deciding what I am going to preach about. One time a young man from the Bible college wanted to interview me. The first question he asked was, "How do you prepare your sermons?"

"Well, first I pray and then I wait upon the Lord until He impresses my heart with what is going to help the most people."

"Now that's the stupidest thing I've ever heard in my life," he responded.

"What do you mean?"

He flipped his Bible in my face and said, "You've got the Word, just preach anything and it will go."

I kept my cool and said, "You take that philosophy if you want, but I'll take mine and wait on the Lord."

He was a cessationist and believed all that is needed is in the Bible. He didn't believe in the guidance of the Holy Spirit. The last I heard, he was working in a pizza parlor.

I was driving along one day and popped in tape number two from my teaching called, "The Day of Global Confusion." I had just preached it a few weeks earlier. As I listened to this message about waiting on the Lord, I couldn't believe how fresh, powerful and prophetic it was. It was like the Holy Spirit was speaking and giving me things to say, and I couldn't remember preparing the message. I think it just came by the rhema revelation of the Lord as I was speaking. It was so good I pulled into the parking lot at Steak 'N' Shake just to listen. I don't say that to be prideful. I was so touched and inspired by God's message, I just clicked my seat to lay back and soaked it up.

Tenderize Your Heart

As you wait on the Lord, you develop a heart that is sensitive so He can guide you. You're not like a horse pulling this way and that way or like a stubborn old mule that refuses to budge. When your heart is tender, the Lord can guide you gently by His Spirit. In His presence your heart develops sensitivity to His guidance system. Here are a few things that can happen:

- You can be protected from being at the wrong place at the wrong time.

- You can receive direction where you are supposed to be and what you are supposed to do.

- You can be sensitive to the needs of others and speak a word of encouragement into their lives.

- You can speak prophetically at a critical time.

George Wishert, a Scottish saint, preacher and prophet, lived a simple servant's life during the 1500s. The Catholic cardinals hated him and constantly stirred up the people against him. One day he went to a town called Dundee, and no one would listen to him when he preached or prophesied. As George left town that day, he said:

> "God is my witness, I never desired your trouble, but your comfort; ... but I am sure, to reject the word of God and drive away his messengers, is not the way to save you from trouble, but to bring you into it...When I am gone...if it be well with you for a long while, I am not led by the Spirit of truth; but if unexpected troubles come upon you, remember this is the cause, and turn to God by repentance, for he is merciful."[1]

With that word, George Wishert took off on horseback for his home forty miles away.

Four days later a plague broke out in Dundee infecting over half of the city. Communication was slow in those days. It was a month before Wishert heard about the plague in Dundee and returned to the city where he preached the Gospel and ministered to the sick. People received it, and he stayed until every one was healed.

Cardinal Beaten hated Wishert so much that he tried to have him killed on several occasions. The Cardinal swore he would have Wishert burned at the stake as a heretic. One day Wishert received a message that a good friend was ill and needed him to come and pray immediately. Wishert saddled his horse and started riding with two friends. He stopped suddenly and said, "The Holy Spirit is forbidding me to go." He bowed his head and prayed for a while. Then he said, "My friend is not sick. This is a trap Cardinal Beaten has set to try to kill me again." Wishert turned around and went back home while his two friends continued on. Sure enough the Cardinal had an ambush planned down the road.[2]

The Holy Spirit saved Wishert's life. He'll do the same for you if you will wait and listen to His voice. If you wait for the power of the Holy Spirit, not only will you have access to God's guidance system, you will also have His Spirit to guide you through life.

Waiting isn't fun. However, if you want to benefit from God's guidance-on-the-go system, you must develop the right foundation on God's Word. You need to learn the art of waiting on the Lord daily for His promise, His power, and His protection using peace as your umpire. Then follow the direction the Holy Spirit gives you, which is the third key to supernatural guidance.

Chapter 8

Key Number 3: Follow The Holy Spirit's Guidance

During World War II at a morning church service in England, a woman from the congregation ran up and whispered to the pastor, "I just had a vision of the church exploding. It was so real. I wonder if we should get the people out of here?" She gave the word to him quietly for him to judge the vision rather than shouting it out for all to hear.

The pastor knew this woman had a solid foundation in the Word, was a faithful prayer warrior, and knew how to wait on the Lord. Because of her credibility, the pastor trusted her vision and said to the congregation, "We are going to dismiss church a little early today. We would like you to vacate the building and move away from the church as quickly as possible."[1]

The people filed out as directed. Just as everyone was a safe distance from the building, a stray V-2 rocket struck the church, and it exploded in a ball of fire.

What would have happened if this woman had not taken her vision seriously and acted upon it? What would have happened if the pastor had just shrugged it off and not listened to her? How many times do we mull over in our minds a vision or a word from the Lord? We say to ourselves, "Oh, it must be my imagination. Everyone will think I'm crazy if I share this." We cannot afford to let fear or false pride stand in the way of immediate obedience no matter how the Holy Spirit gives direction.

Hear And Obey

We must become true disciples of Jesus, which means to hear and obey without questioning and without arguing. When Jesus called His disciples this is what He said:

> Then He said to them, "Follow Me, and I will make you fishers of men." They *immediately* left *their* nets and followed Him. Going on from there, He saw two other brothers, James *the son* of Zebedee, and John his brother, in the boat with Zebedee their father, mending their nets. He called them, and *immediately* they left the boat and their father, and followed Him.
>
> — Matthew 4:19-22

> As Jesus passed on from there, He saw a man named Matthew sitting at the tax office. And He said to him, "Follow Me." So he arose and followed Him.
>
> — Matthew 9:9

> Then Jesus said to His disciples, "If anyone desires to come after Me, let him deny himself, and take up his cross, and follow Me. "
>
> — Matthew 16:24

Notice the disciples followed Him *immediately*, leaving everything behind. They didn't know how they were going to eat or put clothes on their backs or provide for their families. Each one denied himself, which required true humility. The Amplified Bible says this means to "disregard, lose sight of and forget himself and his own interests." Taking up His cross meant they accepted His calling as their own.

One young man tried to put his own conditions on following Jesus. He wanted to go home and take care of his father until whatever time his father died. Then he would follow the Lord. Jesus told him bluntly:

> Follow Me, and let the dead bury their own dead.
>
> — Matthew 8:22b

If we are going to follow the Holy Spirit's guidance, we must hear and obey immediately just as the early disciples did. God isn't going to wait on us to make up our minds. He expects us to act on what He is showing us without trying to figure it out in our natural minds first.

The Holy Spirit was active in guiding the early church disciples, and we should follow their example as well. Paul and Silas were on a missionary journey intending to go to Asia, but God had a different plan, as we will read.

> Now when they had gone through Phrygia and the region of Galatia, they were forbidden by the Holy Spirit to preach the word in Asia. After they had come to Mysia, they tried to go into Bithynia, but the Spirit did not permit them. So passing by Mysia, they came down to Troas. And a vision appeared to Paul in the night. A man of Macedonia stood and pleaded with him, saying, "Come over to Macedonia and help us." Now after he had seen the vision, immediately we sought to go to Macedonia, concluding that the Lord had called us to preach the gospel to them.
>
> — Acts 16:6-10

Jesus had said to go into all the world and preach the Gospel. These disciples were going to Asia to preach the Gospel, but the Holy Spirit stopped them. Their hearts were pure in what they were trying to do, but Paul knew the importance of immediate obedience. He didn't whine about having to change his plan or wonder whether he was really hearing God. He had a vision and followed the Lord's direction. We don't know if there was danger awaiting them in

Asia. We do know that God had a divine appointment for them in Macedonia and from their obedience a church was birthed in Philippi.

He Still Speaks

The Holy Spirit speaks to us today just as He did to the disciples and people in the early church. One day I was driving down the highway behind a big truck. All of a sudden the Holy Spirit said, "Back off now!" It wasn't an audible voice, but the impression was so strong I stepped on the brake and eased back away from the truck. When I was a safe distance away, one of the truck's rear wheels wobbled off and began bouncing down the highway. If I hadn't listened when the Holy Spirit told me to back off, that wheel would probably have come right through my windshield. The Holy Spirit will protect us if we listen and obey.

Sometimes He speaks in a still small voice down inside us like when He told me to back off from the truck. Other times He may speak through a dream or a vision to guide, lead or teach us. Years ago I had a dream that was so vivid I still remember it clearly.

The church I'm pastor of in Lansing, Michigan, was a 450-seat sanctuary on St. Joseph Highway, and we were having multiple services to handle our growing numbers. God had gloriously blessed us, and we were talking about moving and building a larger building. At first I wasn't sure I wanted to move to a different location. I thought we should stay put and perhaps add on to the building. Then I had the dream.

A Fork In The Road

I was on a big snowmobile with my family. My wife, Mary Jo, was behind me and then my daughter, Trina, and my son, David. They were little then. We were snowmobiling down a road and came to a fork in the road. The road went straight but a fork also veered off to the right. Looking straight ahead and staying on our present course, I could see a beautiful lake all frozen over, rimmed with huge pine trees. It was like a winter wonderland with a soft blanket of fresh snow sparkling in the sunlight. As we approached the fork in the road, I heard the Holy Spirit say, "Turn to the right." I remember looking both ways, but the road to the right took a turn that blocked any view of what might be ahead.

The road straight ahead was familiar and beautiful to the eyes. I drove straight ahead and thought about how much fun it would be to go on the lake and spin around a bit. We flew along the trail with the wind biting our cheeks. I could hear the kids laughing as we slid out onto the ice and spun around and around. Suddenly, the ice cracked and the heavy snowmachine carrying my entire family broke through and sank into the freezing, dark water. I came up gasping for air, searching desperately for my family. Mary Jo was under the water, and all I could see was Trina's little hand reaching out of the water. I tried to grab her but couldn't reach her. I couldn't rescue my own family. That's when I woke up with my heart pounding out of my chest.

Immediately I said, "Lord, was that dream from you? Are you trying to tell me something?" It seemed like the Holy Spirit said, "You'll know soon." I was really frightened.

Mary Jo and I prayed about the dream and felt the Lord say, "Yes, I want you to move the church." I said, "Okay, Lord, I won't argue any longer."

We were looking at some property on Snow Road, which was just down the road from our current property on St. Joseph. Then another piece of property became available on Creyts Road, which was also nearby. I remember going out in the front yard of the church and looking down St. Joseph. That is when I realized Snow Road was to the left and Creyts Road was on the right. It was almost like God took a transparency of that dream and laid it over the roads. If I continued the course that I was going on, it would be disastrous for the church and my family. I knew we were to turn right. We bought the property on Creyts Road and have been happy we did ever since.

Blessings Come Through Obedience

When God speaks, you profit when you listen and obey. God loves you and wants you to prosper by receiving His spiritual, physical, emotional, *and* financial blessings. When Mary Jo and I first started in the pastorate, we didn't make or have a lot of money. One morning I was reading God's Word and came to a Scripture that talked about silver and gold. I felt the Holy Spirit speak to me and say to buy silver. I didn't have any idea how to do it.

About that time John and Karen Yang came to our church. I knew John had some knowledge in investing. I asked what he knew about buying silver. He told me I could go to Liberty Coin and buy a little silver each week. Every payday, I went and bought one silver coin at a cost of four or five dollars. We kept our collection of silver coins in a safe deposit box at the bank. It seemed like a small thing, but I was being obedient to what the Holy Spirit said to do.

Mary Jo and I were living in a little two-bedroom bungalow. With the two kids we were bursting at the seams. There was no play space, so Mary Jo and I turned our bedroom into a playroom. We bought one of those blowup air mattresses and put it on the living room floor each night. The kids had a playroom, and Mary Jo and I slept on the living room floor.

As time went along, we began looking for a larger place, but everything seemed to be financially out of our reach. We talked about building a house, but I didn't feel it was the right thing to do while we were building the House of God. Every week I continued to buy a little bit of silver. Some weeks I could buy five dollars worth and other times maybe ten. After moving the church into the new building, we decided to get more serious about finding a house. I called a realtor friend who said she knew of a house that had just come on the market. She thought we should take a look at it. The property was somewhat overgrown, needed new landscaping and the decorating inside needed updating, but the house was solid.

The minute I saw that house the Holy Spirit said, "Put in an offer." We didn't have to look any further. I asked the Lord how much I should offer and the Lord said, "Make a full-price offer." That very day we made a full-price offer and it was accepted. The "For Sale" sign had only been up for a few hours, but I asked them to take it down.

We had some money from the sale of our little bungalow, but we needed $30,000 for the closing on this house. We were short about $5,000, but by faith we set a closing date. I told them what our down payment would be and made arrangements to finance the rest with the bank. The day of the closing was upon us, and I still didn't have the extra $5,000. I remember crying out to God saying, "God what am I going to do? The closing is only a few hours away, and I've scraped together all I know to scrape. I still need $5,000." All of a sudden I heard the Holy Spirit say one word, "Silver."

We went to the bank and gathered up all the silver coins I had bought over the years. Just a few days before, the price of silver had gone up to eight dollars an ounce. We sold the silver. Not only did we come up with the $5,000 we lacked to close on the house, but there was enough to make our missions' pledge, pay our taxes, and buy everything else we needed for the new house. I listened to the voice of the Holy Spirit, and we prospered as a result of our obedience.

God's desire is to guide you in every arena of life. It takes humility, knowledge of His written Word, a time of waiting, and then obedience to His guidance, but the rewards are magnificent. God has given us His guidance-on-the-go system. It is up to us to apply it in our daily walk with Him. God holds the map to guide you on your journey.

Chapter 9

God Holds The Map To Guide You

Long after a war is over, danger often lurks in grassy meadows, on forgotten dusty roadways, or in deserted rice paddies. Innocent children and unsuspecting adults are maimed or killed after stepping on unmarked land mines left behind by the armies that once fought over the territory.

How many times have we seen pictures on TV of precious children with one or both legs missing because they went out to play and unknowingly tripped the wire on a hidden land mine? How many farmers have lost limbs as they cleared their fields to plant a desperately needed crop?

Often these crippled victims are from poor countries, and all they have are handmade crutches cut from tree branches. Some have to just scoot along the ground using their hands to propel them. Many are left begging on the streets and struggling to survive because they couldn't detect the impending danger.

I was watching a documentary on the Discovery Channel one night about an East African nation where over seven hundred people die each year from snake-bites. They may be just walking along a path, and suddenly a snake strikes from the underbrush. The lightning speed of the bite is unexpected. Death comes within minutes.

We may sympathize with such victims on TV, but few of us can actually relate to the danger of land mines in our back yards, or deadly snakes whose venom kills before there is time to obtain an antidote. However, in the spiritual and emotional realms we encounter land mines and snake pits that can be equally as crippling and deadly. There are no red flags flying above them to warn us of impending danger.

For example, consider a young woman who falls in love with a handsome, church-going man only to discover too late she has married "Dr. Jekyll and Mr. Hyde." On the outside he looks like the picture-perfect, loving Christian husband, but at home he is physically and verbally abusive to her. She cries herself to sleep at night wondering how she could have been so wrong. The problem was she didn't pick up on the impending danger when his college roommate tried to warn her that her future husband wasn't all he appeared to be. She was "in love" and didn't inquire of the Lord or seek wise counsel about the warning.

Imagine how many lives could have been saved if people living in the land mine areas and snake-infested locations, were given detailed maps to guide them around the mines and pointed out snake pits in the underbrush! How many times could we avoid emotional land mines, snares, and the spiritual snakes in our lives if we simply used God's guidance-on-the-go system — allowing the Holy Spirit to guide us around the traps and danger spots on to a safe route?

His Map Is Marked

The Holy Spirit has the map of your life laid out before Him. He knows the beginning from the end, and He is the only one who can light your path. He knows where the land mines are located and sees the snakes waiting in the underbrush. God is just waiting for you to humble yourself and ask Him to guide and direct your footsteps. It says so in this Scripture:

> Trust in the LORD with all your heart, and lean not on your own understanding; In all your ways

> acknowledge Him, and He shall direct your
> paths.
>
> — Proverbs 3:5,6

Some of you who are reading this book have been critically wounded by emotional land mines. You've been hurt and rejected, and the serpent's bite has poisoned you with anger and bitterness. God sees where you have been and where you are, and He wants to heal you and direct you onto a safer path.

Trust Him with Everything

Every promise of God requires obedient action to be taken. The above Scripture first and foremost requires you to *trust* God with *all* your heart. There is no room for doubt and second guessing God in this scenario. It requires an "all-or-nothing," "sold-out to God" kind of attitude.

The next key requirement is to stop trying to figure it out in your own logical mind. If you had full understanding of the situation you wouldn't need His help, but you don't, so get out of His way.

Lastly, you must acknowledge Who He is — the Lord God Almighty, the Truth and the Light — and submit *everything* in your life totally and completely to Him. "All" means exactly what it says, "all." That means you are to inquire of Him and seek His guidance in *everything* you do, not just when times are tough.

When you start going your own way, danger awaits. God is just waiting for you to ask; then He will lead you on a straight, safe path. God will guide you around the land mines that may hurt or cripple you emotionally or spiritually, and shield you from the snakes waiting to inject you with anger, unforgiveness, and bitterness along the way.

Hebrew words paint pictures that take the meaning further than any literal translation. The Hebrew word, "yashar," for the word, "direct," found in Proverbs 3:6, means "to be straight or even, to make right, pleasant or prosperous."[1] This Hebrew word refers to "the shortest distance between two points." In other words, if you ask Him, God will take you along the most direct route between point A and point B that avoids the land mines and snake pits.

It takes many hours of studying, training and experience before a pilot qualifies for a license. Likewise, learning to hear the voice of the Holy Spirit doesn't come naturally. It takes many hours of soaking up the knowledge and wisdom of the Word of God, developing an intimacy with the Lord, and practicing the art of hearing His voice clearly to learn how to use His guidance-on-the-go system.

I keep emphasizing this, but it is so critical to understand we are living in dangerous times. It is more important now to hear the voice of the Holy Spirit than it ever has been in the past. *Now* is the time to get your training and on-the-job experience. That's why in the next two chapters I am going to discuss why these two principles of God's guidance are so important:

1. We are absolutely incapable of directing our own lives.

2. God loves us deeply and *wants* to give us direction.

Chapter 10

Guidance Principle Number 1: We Are Incapable Of Guiding Our Own Lives

Do you believe you are capable of guiding your own life? If you answered this question with a "yes," I can tell you danger is ahead. When we leave God out of the picture, there is no way we can steer clear of the land mines and snake pits the enemy puts in our path. Just like a pilot who tries to fly without his FAR/AIM manual and guidance systems, we are destined to crash and burn when we try to live without God's instruction manual — the Bible — and His guidance-on-the-go system provided through the Holy Spirit.

We can read in the Bible how the people of Israel did this over and over again. It is no different today than it was in ancient biblical days. When we don't listen to the voice of God and follow His direction trouble comes knocking at our door. Things may seem to be going great, but eventually the sin of rebellion brings defeat.

The Roaring Twenties

In his book, *The Great Crash of 1929*, John Galbreath tells the story of eight men who controlled more wealth than there was in the whole US treasury. The stock market was climbing to an all time high and there was money to be made. I remember seeing a TV documentary about one of these men, Jessie Livermore, who was a great Wall Street bear in the 1920's. The film showed him smoking his big cigar and bragging about the lavish, opulent lifestyle he was living, with a fleet of fancy cars and beautiful homes.

The book and the documentary talked about a meeting these men held at the Edgewater Beach Hotel in Chicago in 1923. Jessie Livermore, Charles Schwab, and six other men arrogantly followed the charts, cycles and trends of Wall Street, and directed their own paths oblivious to the pending danger.

Then came October 29, 1929. Within months three or four of these powerful men committed suicide because they had become paupers overnight. Two others landed in prison, and the others died penniless because they didn't foresee what was coming. They didn't harken to the voice of the Lord or abide in His Word, and judgment came.

Destined For A Crash

These wealthy men were not the only ones who lost all they had. Many ordinary people jumped on the bandwagon and saw there was *easy* money to be made in the bull market of the '20s. Some invested all the savings they had buying unit trusts, which today are known as mutual funds. Everyone thought the lucrative market would go on and on.

I'm sure there were a few lone prophets of that day crying out that judgment was at hand; but for the most part no one was listening. The crash that followed plunged the entire country into "The Great Depression."

This sounds familiar, doesn't it? With all the ups and downs on Wall Street, many still believe it can't happen again. If you are day trading or playing the market today, you'd better be listening to the voice of the Lord. The Lord's prophets are speaking. Are you heeding their warning?

Listen To The Voice Of The Prophet

In the twenty-seventh chapter of Acts, the apostle Paul was a prisoner being taken to Rome by a Roman centurion. They were on board a ship getting ready to sail when the Lord told Paul they should not leave the port yet because there would be a great disaster and loss of life if they did. The centurion went to the ship's helmsman and owner and shared what Paul had said.

However, he was persuaded they should proceed anyway. As they left the island, a soft wind blew from the south and everything seemed to be going fine.

Then they encountered a storm of typhoon proportions. It raged on for days. The ship's crew and passengers did all they could to battle the storm, but it appeared all hope was gone and the ship would be lost.

Paul spoke up again and said:

> "Men, you should have taken my advice not to sail from Crete; then you would have spared yourselves this damage and loss. But now I urge you to keep up your courage, because not one of you will be lost; only the ship will be destroyed. Last night an angel of the God whose I am and whom I serve stood beside me and said, `Do not be afraid, Paul. You must stand trial before Caesar; and God has graciously given you the lives of all who sail with you.' So keep up your courage, men, for I have faith in God that it will hap-

pen just as he told me. Nevertheless, we must
run aground on some island."

— Acts 27:21b-26 (NIV)

Along the North African coast there are sandbars
made of quicksand. If a ship is caught in one of these
sandbars, the quicksand swallows it up. Anyone trying to jump overboard gets caught in the quicksand,
as do any lifeboats. There appeared to be no way out
for Paul and his fellow passengers, but Paul was saying to the others on the ship, "We're going to make it
through this safely. Just hold steady." But a couple of
men decided to try to secretly abandon ship. Now,
Paul was a prisoner, but the centurion and the soldiers listened to him this time when he warned:

"Unless these men stay with the ship, you cannot be saved."

— Acts 27:31b (NIV)

Total obedience was required, and the centurion
and soldiers stopped these men from leaving the
ship. Paul proceeded to give everyone specific instructions to eat so they would be strengthened, and
when the ship ran aground while still a ways off
shore, everyone swam or floated to shore on pieces
of wreckage. Not one life was lost because they listened to the voice of God's prophet.

Beware Of The Quicksand

Without God's guidance we are a ready target for the devil's wiles and schemes — his quicksand. He shoots his fiery darts and, without our faith shield in place, we get off the path and into trouble. His little fiery dart may be a lustful thought that encourages someone to look at pornography. Or it may be a voice saying, "You can make lots of money doing this. Don't worry; just think of all the extra money you can give to the church." It sounds harmless especially when there is some spiritual benefit attached, but the bottom line is he has just inflamed you with a fiery dart of greed or covetousness.

A couple spoke with me one time about a motivational speaker with whom they had gotten involved. He is an energetic, very charismatic man who smiles all the time and makes his infomercials sound like a lot of fun. This couple joined his group of followers and began investing more and more money into his "self-help" products and seminars. Before long they were even walking barefoot on hot coals.

Actually, he was leading them into a form of Hinduism. Thank the Lord, God saved them and filled them with His Holy Spirit before they got into it any further. He said to them, "I'm getting you off this land. I'm going to clean you up, heal you and get you on the right path."

Watch Out For The Big, Bad Wolf

When we try to direct our own path, we may fall into the trap of listening to the wrong voices. Sometimes the wolf is dressed in sheep's clothing and his voice sounds very spiritual. Believe it or not, sometimes it even comes from the pulpit. It happened in biblical times so what makes us think it doesn't happen today? Let's read what Jeremiah had to say about it:

> For this is what the LORD says: "At this time I will hurl out those who live in this land; I will bring distress on them so that they may be captured."

> Woe to me because of my injury! My wound is incurable! Yet I said to myself, "This is my sickness, and I must endure it." My tent is destroyed; all its ropes are snapped. My sons are gone from me and are no more; no one is left now to pitch my tent or to set up my shelter. The shepherds are senseless and do not inquire of the LORD; so they do not prosper and all their flock is scattered. Listen! The report is coming— a great commotion from the land of the north! It will make the towns of Judah desolate, a haunt of jackals.

> I know, O LORD, that a man's life is not his own; it is not for man to direct his steps. Correct me, LORD, but only with justice—not in your anger, lest you reduce me to nothing. Pour out your wrath on the nations that do not acknowledge you, on the peoples who do not call on your name. For they have devoured Jacob; they have

> devoured him completely and destroyed his
> homeland.
>
> — Jeremiah 10:18-25 (NIV)

In this same Scripture in the King James version
verse 21 says:

> For the pastors are become brutish, and have
> not sought the LORD: therefore they shall not
> prosper, and all their flocks shall be scattered.
>
> — Jeremiah 10:21 (KJV)

The word "brutish" in Hebrew means "animal-
like with no spiritual sense."[1]

I have a dog that is interested in only two things,
food and attention. She'll do a trick if I give her food.
She'll beg at the table for "people food," and it doesn't
matter if she just ate a whole bowl of dog food. She'll
rub up against me and lick my hand to get me to pay
attention to her. If I ignore her, she will get mad and
go behind a chair. Brutish people act the same way.

Pastors are responsible for feeding their flock.
When they become brutish they become self-cen-
tered, thinking only of their own appetites, their own
prosperity, and the things that appeal to them. In other
words, they no longer hear from God; and so they
don't speak the Word of God or interpret it correctly
for their flock — just like in Jeremiah's day.

There are a lot of crippled, wounded Christians
— including church leaders — who walk with spiri-

tual crutches because they didn't listen to the voice of the Lord, and were abused and hurt in the church. Some have walked away from God completely. I call these the walking wounded.

Don't Be A War Casualty

Your life is not your own and you can't direct your own steps. You can not get from point A to point B by yourself without becoming a casualty of war. What happened in Jeremiah's day is happening today, and judgment can come just as quickly as it did back then ... Overnight.

Judah was a mighty nation feared by all the surrounding nations. However, in the middle of the night disaster struck and the people were taken into captivity. Don't be lulled into a false sense of security. Overnight bank accounts, brokerage houses and retirement accounts can be drained. The enemy can take everything suddenly.

God, however, is going to prosper His people, but it will only be those who are seeking Him and listening to His voice. Others will be judged right along with the rest of the world.

It grieves God to have to chastise His people, but He does it for our own good. He knows how far off course we can wander without Him, and when we get too far off the path, He pulls us back however He has to do it. It may hurt at the time, but it is for our own protection. Pray that He does it with justice and not anger. Welcome His correction.

God knows we can't direct our own paths, and He is just waiting to guide and direct us. He loves us so much that He gave us His Holy Spirit to provide us with the guidance and direction. We need His instruction to keep us out of the mine field and away from the snake pits of life. Keep reading and you'll discover just how deep His love is for you.

Chapter 11

Guidance Principle #2: God Loves You Deeply and *Wants* to Give You Direction

Living by *your* master plan instead of waiting on God for His master plan takes you into dangerous territory. I hope by now you realize you aren't capable of directing your own life. You can move more quickly from point A, where you are — to point B, where you desire and need to be — if you stop trying to do it your way. God wants to be involved in your life, and He loves you so much He made every provision for you to live a happy, prosperous life. The problem is many believers can't comprehend how incredible God's love for them is, as we will read in the following story:

Christine had been sexually abused as a little girl and hated men. She turned to a lesbian lifestyle. She never wore makeup or nail polish, and she cut her hair short and dressed like a man. She wanted to be as "butch" as possible.

One time, someone told her about a conference where a lot of former homosexuals ministered. Christine decided to attend, but only for the purpose of ridiculing those who were ministering. She did not know this was a divine appointment that would change her life forever.

A well-known worship leader and songwriter who had been delivered out of homosexuality gave his testimony that night about how God delivered him from perverted sexual urges and impulses of homosexuality. The Holy Spirit pricked Christine's heart that night, and for the first time in her life, she felt hope spring to life in her spirit. She came forward and gave her life to Jesus.

A number of former homosexuals and lesbians who had been saved under this ministry were cosmetologists. They understood how important it was to change the outward appearance of the lesbians who were being saved at the meetings. They set up booths, and right after the service they took the new converts through a process of styling their hair, giving them a manicure and a complete make-over with makeup and new clothes.

Christine was so excited to discover Jesus loved her enough to save her that her heart was softened. The love of Jesus was ministered to her as she was guided from booth to booth, receiving first class treatment. She had never had her nails done before, and they felt heavy from the nail polish. Her new hairstyle softened her facial features, and makeup added to the glow of Jesus on her countenance. Colorful, feminine clothes and pretty earrings finished the make-over. When they led her to look in a full-length mirror, Christine didn't recognize the woman looking back at her.

When the conference reconvened, the emcee announced, "Ladies and gentlemen, we are going to introduce someone who got a new start in Jesus today. I present to you, 'Christine.'" She walked out on the platform in her new dress and make-over feeling a bit intimidated until everyone started applauding and someone yelled, "Christine, you're beautiful!" Others joined in the chorus. She broke down and cried because people had said a lot of things to her in life, but no one had ever told her she was beautiful. She cried and cried. As she went backstage, she looked in the mirror again and said, "I *am* beautiful. I *am* beautiful. God, thank you that I am beautiful!"

Christine never went back to that lesbian lifestyle. She is serving God and giving her testimony whenever she can. She went from looking like a rugged man to a beautiful woman. She was transformed by the love of Christ; first on the inside, then on the outside. She heard God's voice and discovered the depth of His love. She allowed Him to direct her path and found a whole new life.

The Cross = Love

One of the reasons people can't comprehend the depth of God's love is because they don't understand the power of the Cross. It is the key to victorious living; knowing Him and walking in the calling and fullness of our destiny. The Cross represents the love of God as we read in these Scriptures:

> For God so loved the world that he gave his one and only Son, that whoever believes in him shall not perish but have eternal life.
>
> — John 3:16 (NIV)

> But because of his great love for us, God, who is rich in mercy, made us alive with Christ even when we were dead in transgressions — it is by grace you have been saved.
>
> —Ephesians 2:4,5 (NIV)

> But God demonstrates his own love for us in
> this: While we were still sinners, Christ died for
> us.
>
> —Romans 5:8 (NIV)

God sent His most treasured possession – His only Son – to take our sins upon Him and die in our place. That is how much He loves us. Every time we see a cross we should think of His love.[1]

A Love Song

Psalm 32 is a beautiful romantic song that speaks of how deep God's love is for us. Let's read it in The Living Bible:

> What happiness for those whose guilt has been forgiven! What joys when sins are covered over! What relief for those who have confessed their sins and God has cleared their record.
>
> There was a time when I wouldn't admit what a sinner I was. But my dishonesty made me miserable and filled my days with frustration. All day and all night your hand was heavy on me. My strength evaporated like water on a sunny day until I finally admitted all my sins to you and stopped trying to hide them. I said to myself, "I will confess them to the Lord." And you forgave me! All my guilt is gone.
>
> Now I say that each believer should confess his sins to God when he is aware of them, while there is time to be forgiven. Judgment will not touch him if he does.
>
> You are my hiding place from every storm of life; you even keep me from getting into trouble! You surround me with songs of victory. I will

> instruct you (says the Lord) and guide you along the best pathway for your life; I will advise you and watch your progress. Don't be like a senseless horse or mule that has to have a bit in its mouth to keep it in line!
>
> Many sorrows come to the wicked, but abiding love surrounds those who trust in the Lord. So rejoice in him, all those who are his, and shout for joy, all those who try to obey him.
>
> —Psalm 32 1-11 (TLB)

When you come to Jesus, all your sin is charged to His account instead of your account. By confessing and repenting of your sin, it is covered by Jesus' blood and God no longer sees it. What a relief it is to know your record is cleared. No longer do you need to struggle and be sucked down by the quicksand of sin.

I sense in my spirit that some of you reading this book may be carrying unconfessed sin in your hearts. Are you feeling the heaviness of God's hand on you? If so, it's because you have a divine appointment with destiny today. God led you to this book and placed His heavy hand upon you so He could pull you off a land mine you are about to step on.

Stop right now and openly confess out loud any sin you have been hiding. God already knows about it. He wants to clear your record. Your repentance and obedience will stop His judgment and remove the guilt you have been carrying.

If this is what you have been feeling, pray this prayer:

> "Lord, I confess I've been doing my own thing. Snakes have bitten me and I'm filled with anger and the venom of bitterness. I have fallen into a trap from which I can't seem to escape. I've been struck by an emotional or spiritual land mine, and I'm hurting. I've tried to direct and guide my own life, but Your Word says that is impossible. I need You as my Savior. I ask You to come into my heart and cleanse me of all of my sins. I need You to guide my life."

Welcome to the family of God! You are now a King's kid and your sins are washed away! From now on you have direct access to the King of Kings and the Lord of Lords. You are no longer alone... The Lord is now your hiding place in the midst of storms and trouble because He loves YOU!

Here is my paraphrase of what David said in Psalm 32:7: "Lord, you're my hiding place. You keep me from getting into trouble, stepping on land mines, being bitten by snakes and falling into quicksand. You surround me with songs of victory." If that isn't incredible love, I don't know what else it could be called.

Let's go back and read verse eight in the King James, so we can look at the Hebrew translation for some of the words:

> I will instruct thee and teach thee in the way
> which thou shalt go; I will guide thee with mine
> eye.
>
> —Psalm 32:8

The Hebrew word for "instruct" is "sakal," which means to be intelligent, act wisely, guide wittingly or to have insight.[2] In other words, God is going to give you "street smarts." You're going to walk through that jungle and know some things you have no way of knowing in a natural sense. People around you may say, "How does he know that? Has he been in this jungle before?"

In our English language we use the words "teach" and "instruct" interchangeably, but in the Hebrew they are two distinctly different words. The Hebrew word for "teach" in this verse is "yarah." It means, "to point out as if by aiming a finger, or to throw like shooting an arrow."[3]

Have you ever had a parent or a teacher point or shake a finger in your face and say, "Listen to me. I'm going to teach you a lesson?" In other words, God is going to give you a little correction as you walk along life's path as He says, "Turn right here or go left there, because there is a land mine ahead that I want you to miss."

The Hebrew word for "guide" is "ya`ats," which means, "to advise, to consult, to give counsel, to purpose, to devise, to plan."[4] God is saying, "I'm going to watch over you like I'm looking down from the top and make sure you don't get caught in any snares the enemy has laid for you. I will give you counsel which way to go." As you put your trust in God, His abiding love will surround you. That is an awesome promise.

God guides us in many different ways, all of which are in harmony with His Word. We are going to examine four ways God guides us:

1. Prophetic words

2. Dreams and visions

3. Hearing or reading an anointed Word

4. Through other people (the mouth of two or three witnesses)

Prophetic Words

In Bible School as a young man I was taught the roles of the prophet and the apostle had only been for the early church. Therefore, I didn't think there was any such thing as a prophet or an apostle in our time. Then my wife, Mary Jo, and I went to a conference at Christ for the Nations Institute in Dallas, Texas. One of the speakers was Chuck Flynn who was said to be a prophet.

At one of his meetings, we were told if we wanted to be prophesied over to stand in line after the service. Mary Jo and I got in line just to see what it was all about. She was pregnant and had been experiencing terrible back pains.

When it was our turn, Chuck Flynn put his hand on Mary Jo's back and said, "Father, heal this back pain right now." He had no way of knowing about her back pain, and the pain disappeared. Then he said to me, "Your ministry is about to take a change but don't fear that change." He told me of some of the opposition and resistance I would experience and how to keep focused on the prize that was set before me. In five minutes the things he told me spanned a seven-year period in my future.

At that time, we were running the Good Ground Evangelical Association that included radio programming and a biblical correspondence course. I always wanted to be a teacher and evangelist, go into different cities, teach the people, get them saved, and then leave town as quickly as possible.

Being a pastor was *not* part of my vision because a pastor had to do all of the finish work like, developing courses, providing discipleship, getting people cleaned up, changing their spiritual diapers and things like that. My vision was to go into a town, stir things up, and leave the mess for the church's pastor to clean up.

Right after Mary Jo and I returned to Lansing, Michigan from the conference in Dallas, my pastor came and asked if I could be interested in becoming a pastor. Chuck Flynn's words came to my mind, "Don't be afraid; your ministry is about to change." And now the rest is history. Everything played out just the way this prophet said it would happen.

I have seen the prophetic operate many times since those early days, and I believe it is one way God speaks and provides guidance to His people.

Dreams And Visions

Some people are afraid of dreams and visions because they don't understand how they can come from God. The devil has taken these legitimate tools God gave His people to guide and direct them, and perverted them through the occult. We shouldn't let what the devil has perverted scare us from being guided by dreams and visions from the Lord.

Visualization is nothing more than biblical meditation on the words and works of God. In a vision you are simply seeing with your eye of faith, the promises of God becoming reality in your life. Jesus was trying to get His disciples to visualize the souls ready to be saved when He told them to: "look on the fields; they are ripe for harvest."

Dreams and visions are for today as we read in the following Scripture, which itself is a direct quote from Joel 2:28 in the Old Testament. Peter was preaching on the day of Pentecost and said:

> **In the last days, God says, I will pour out my Spirit on all people. Your sons and daughters will prophesy, your young men will see visions, your old men will dream dreams.**
>
> **Even on my servants, both men and women, I will pour out my Spirit in those days, and they will prophesy.**
>
> —Acts 2:17,18 (NIV)

I have seen visions and dreamed dreams so I don't know if that makes me young or old, but I know they were from the Lord. They have deeply impacted my life. Let me share one such dream.

I was praying one time and fell asleep. That happens to the best of us at times. Well, I dreamed I was walking along a railroad track and the voice of the Lord said, "These are the tracks I have laid out for your life, don't be afraid to follow them."

I saw no problem in this. There was a lot of open space as I walked down the track. I knew that if a train came along I would just hop off the tracks, let it pass on by and then get back on the tracks again.

In the dream I came to a tunnel, and knew intuitively that the tunnel was only wide enough for a train. There was no room for a pedestrian to walk beside the train, going through the tunnel.

I stopped at the opening and peered into the darkness to see if I could see any light at the end of the tunnel. It must have curved because I couldn't see the tunnel's exit. I stood there thinking about whether I should follow the track through the tunnel or climb over the mountain and pick up the tracks on the other side. Again I heard the Lord's voice say, "David, these are the tracks I have laid out for your life; don't be afraid to follow them."

I said, "Okay, Lord, I'm trying not to be afraid." I started walking on the tracks into the tunnel and I remember thinking, *I hope a train doesn't come because I know this tunnel is only big enough for a train. A pedestrian would be turned into hamburger meat if a train came through at the same time.*

The walls of the tunnel were straight and smooth with no indentations. There must have been some light because I could see where I was walking. I was about halfway through the tunnel when I noticed I could see a small shaft of light at the end of the tunnel. I was in this tunnel seemingly alone and, suddenly, I felt the earth start to tremble under my feet.

Have You Heard From The Lord Lately?

I leaned over and put my hand on the rails of the track and sure enough, it was vibrating. A train was coming. I knew there wasn't time to turn around and run back the way I had come. By then I could see the light on the front of the engine, so running forward was not an option. Frantically I looked around for a place to hide, but there was only an inch or two of space between the train and the wall of the tunnel. I was trapped.

My heart was pounding out of my chest and I was sweating. I was scared. I thought maybe I could lie down in the middle of the tracks and let the train pass over me. However, as the train came closer I could see the big cowcatcher on the front that would tear me to pieces. There was nothing I could do.

The train was only a few feet away and I remember pushing myself against the wall of the tunnel screaming, "JESUS!" Just as the train reached me I felt two hands reach out and grab me around the chest, pulling me back into the wall where previously there was no door or indentation. It was like I was standing inside the wall as the train rumbled past me, and I said, "Thank you, Jesus!"

The voice came to me again and said, "Don't be afraid to follow the tracks I've laid down for your life, because when it seems like there is no way, I will make a way for I AM the Way!"

138

The hands released me and I stepped back out into the tunnel. I looked back and there was no indentation or doorway in the wall. I had experienced a miracle. I continued to walk with more confidence down that railroad track, and out of the tunnel.

That dream is as real to me today as the day I experienced it. The Lord wanted me to know He had prepared the way for me and would be my hiding place if I needed it. Whenever I am tempted to waver in my walk with the Lord, I remember that dream. It was a turning point in my life. We will talk more about dreams and visions a bit later in the book.

The Anointed Word

Have you ever gone to church and felt like the pastor had been reading your mail? The message he was preaching just seemed to speak directly to your circumstances at the moment. That's an anointed Word from the Lord, and you need to receive it and be guided by it. You weren't the only one who may have needed that message, but you can be thankful the pastor heard from the Lord as he prepared his sermon.

Sometimes you may have questions about something you have read in the Bible and the answer comes through a message you hear at church, or on a video or cassette tape, or even through an anointed book. God's guidance is not limited to any one avenue of communication, so be open to hear in the most unexpected ways.

As we have already discussed, the Bible is God's *Living Word*. It is life-giving and life-changing. Consider Ron Cun who was a member of the dreaded Purple Gang during the 1920s.

Ron was given an assignment to kill someone but was arrested before he fulfilled the contract. During his seventeen years in prison, the only thing he had to read was a Gideon Bible. One day as he was reading chapters three and four in the book of John, he said it was as if someone was speaking directly to him about how much God loved him. The words on the pages began to flash like a neon sign, and he accepted Jesus as his Savior. Ron's life was transformed.

Through Other People

Sometimes the Lord uses other people to speak truth into our lives. I experienced this when I sang on one of our music CDs, "Heaven at the Hope."

Track number seven, "Almost to Glory" is my song. It has a catchy tune and the music and background singers are great. The truth of the matter was that I heard it before all the music and back-up singing was added, and my singing was pretty sorry. However, as people started coming up and telling me how good my song was, I began to believe it myself.

One day on the way to the office I was listening to the album in the car and thought my song sounded pretty good. I began toying with the thought of doing a whole album, maybe a collection of country hymns. I said, "Lord, just let me know if I ought to make an album. We've got great backup singers and good musicians who could help me."

I came into the office and stopped at the coffeepot in the kitchen. A friend was sitting there and she said, "Oh, Pastor Dave, I bought "Heaven at the Hope" and listened to it for the first time yesterday. I heard your song too."

I thought, *Okay, here it comes again.*

"The best I can say is you kind of sound like Johnny Cash. Pastor, I want you to know I love you, but you're no singer."

Boy did she burst my bubble! As I walked back to my office, I said, "Thank you, Lord, for that guidance and for quickly directing my footsteps." I could have wasted a lot of time and money on a mediocre album because I had allowed pride to cloud the truth.

God is Always There!

God doesn't keep a record and cut you off if you don't quite measure up to His expectations. He doesn't put you off for months and months. He makes a way for you and rewards you for diligently seeking Him.

I have flown almost a million miles with Northwest Airlines. They are my chief carrier when I travel. In 1999 I received a letter from them saying, "Dear Mr. Williams, we are sorry to inform you that you did not qualify to be a 1999 preferred customer."

I like the perks and bonuses of being a preferred customer such as paying coach fare and being upgraded to first class for no extra charge. The problem was the pilots had been on strike that year and I often had to fly other airlines. That had cut down my frequent flyer miles on Northwest, and I barely missed the cutoff as a preferred customer.

After so many frequent flyer miles you can qualify for world perks awards. I decided to use some of my accumulated miles to get free tickets for a trip Mary Jo and I were planning to go to Hawaii. When I went to book the flights, I was told I had to book nine months in advance. Actually, I booked the flights in November for the following November in order to get the seats.

God loves us so much He wants to protect us and guide us. The best part of it is He is always readily available to talk to us or to answer our questions. We don't have to make an appointment months in advance to talk to Him. He never puts us on hold or disconnects from us.

One time I had to change my flight schedule for a trip I had already ticketed. I called the customer service line and got that message, "All of our customer service representatives are busy with other customers now. Your call is important to us. Please hold and the next representative will be with you as soon as possible." I stayed on the line and listened to all the advertisements for vacation getaways, etc.

Every few minutes the customer service message would be repeated reassuring me that my call was important to them. I waited and waited. Then I heard this click and the message changed to, "If you wish to make a domestic reservation, push one. If you wish to make an international reservation, push two. If you would like to know your world perks account balance, press three, etc. I pushed the button I thought was appropriate because I needed to cancel one flight and book two additional flights. Again I hear, "We're sorry all of our customer service representatives are busy with other customers . . .."

All morning I kept trying to get through holding on the line for twenty minutes or more each time. I'm thinking, *I have almost a million miles with this airline. Couldn't they give me a secret number so I could get through?* Over and over I called and waited on hold. Then I heard a click and thought finally, I'm getting through. There were no more advertisements or messages, just a click and nothing. The line went dead. I kept calling until it was time to leave for the airport. I ended up having to fly with two different airlines to make both legs of my trip, because I couldn't get through on the phone.

When you want to talk to God, you're never going to get a busy signal or a voice mail. He is available twenty-four hours a day, seven days a week to guide and teach you. He will keep you from the land mines of life if you have an ear to hear what the Spirit is saying. Have you heard from the Lord lately? Do you know His voice?

Chapter 12

Knowing The Shepherd's Voice

Charles Spurgeon was a powerful preacher in the 1800s. Before each service, he prayed that God would speak to him while he was preaching. One night he stopped in the middle of his sermon and said, "There's a shoemaker in the service tonight. You keep your shop open on the Sabbath day. You were open today and made nine pence. Your profit was four pence, and you sold your soul to the devil for four pence."[1]

The shoemaker later told a missionary, he knew it was God speaking to his soul, and he started closing his shop on Sundays. He was drawn back to listen to Spurgeon again and was led to a saving faith in Jesus Christ.[2]

How did Charles Spurgeon know there was a shoemaker in the audience who kept his shop open on Sunday and made nine pence with a four-pence profit? It was because the Spirit of the Lord spoke to him, and Charles knew the Lord's voice.

Jesus — The Good Shepherd

Throughout the Scriptures God speaks of His people as sheep. Jesus spoke often of His sheep and His role as their Shepherd, as we can read here:

> Most assuredly, I say to you, he who does not enter the sheepfold by the door, but climbs up some other way, the same is a thief and a robber. But he who enters by the door is the shepherd of the sheep. To him the doorkeeper opens, and the sheep hear his voice; and he calls his own sheep by name and leads them out. And when he brings out his own sheep, he goes before them; and the sheep follow him, for they know his voice. Yet they will by no means follow a stranger, but will flee from him, for they do not know the voice of strangers.
>
> —John 10:1-5

> My sheep hear My voice, and I know them, and they follow Me.
>
> —John 10:27

Jesus was saying that He is the *only* door by which His sheep may enter, be saved, and go in and out to pasture. Only His sheep will hear His voice and not be betrayed by another, because sheep know their shepherd and recognize his voice.

Two shepherds decided to feed and water their flocks together because it would be more efficient. Sheep all look alike and, because of their thick wool, it is impossible to brand them to identify their owner, like is done with cattle.

How did the shepherds separate their flocks when it was time to take them home? It was very simple. One of the shepherds stood up on a hillside and began calling to his sheep. All the sheep that were part of his flock came running to him because they knew their shepherd's voice. He then led them home.

In these days we must be able to distinguish the voice of the true Shepherd. One way to tell is that salvation — eternal, abundant life for His sheep — is His first priority. Also, He is willing to give His own life for His sheep, and He doesn't flee and leave His sheep alone to be scattered when a wolf comes. Lastly, He knows or has an intimate relationship with God the Father.

Good Shepherd Or Hireling?

Jesus spoke of the difference between a good shepherd and a hireling in John, chapter 10:

> **The thief does not come except to steal, and to kill, and to destroy. I have come that they may**

> have life, and that they may have *it* more abun-
> dantly. I am the good shepherd. The good shep-
> herd gives His life for the sheep. But a hireling,
> *he who is* not the shepherd, one who does not
> own the sheep, sees the wolf coming and leaves
> the sheep and flees; and the wolf catches the
> sheep and scatters them. The hireling flees be-
> cause he is a hireling and does not care about
> the sheep. I am the good shepherd; and I know
> My *sheep*, and am known by My own. As the
> Father knows Me, even so I know the Father;
> and I lay down My life for the sheep.
>
> —John 10:10-15

I hate to say this but sheep are pretty dumb animals. Sometimes sheep can be tricked into following
another that is not of their own flock. In the stock-
yards farmers that raise sheep for slaughter instead
of wool use what is called a "Judas" sheep to lead
the sheep into the slaughterhouse. The "Judas" sheep
is trained to do the work of a Judas, a betrayer. He is
usually a large sheep that displays an authoritative
manner. The "Judas" sheep is put into the stock pen,
and pretty soon the sheep begin to trust him as he
gains their confidence.

When it is time for slaughter, the "Judas" sheep
leads the entire flock to the chute that goes from the
stockyard pen into the slaughterhouse. Just before
he gets to the doorway to the slaughterhouse, the "Judas" sheep steps aside and oversees all the other
sheep going to their slaughter, their death.

A "Judas" sheep is like the hireling of which Jesus spoke. He is trained in a profession and hired for a job to which he has no calling. He doesn't care anything for the sheep and eventually leads them to their death.

In the Scriptures the word pastor and shepherd are interchangeable. Therefore, a pastor should emulate the characteristics of a good shepherd, not a hireling. Unfortunately, some pastors have gone to seminary and seemingly have all the right credentials, but they are hirelings. Being a pastor is simply a profession that pays a salary and gives them a prestigious title. However, they haven't been called by the Lord to be a pastor. Therefore, they don't have any love for the sheep in their congregation. When the going gets tough or a wolf comes into the church stirring up trouble, the hireling jumps ship and moves on to another church.

A True Shepherd Stirs Controversy

A true shepherd stays through thick and thin to protect the sheep because he has a calling. He has heard the voice of the Lord and is an under-shepherd of the Master Shepherd, Jesus Christ. A true shepherd knows that when he speaks by the Spirit of God, controversy will be stirred up from the sheep that don't have ears to hear. Jesus experienced this every time He spoke to the "religious" leaders of His day because they couldn't understand what He was saying. Here is what He said to them:

> And other sheep I have which are not of this fold; them also I must bring, and they will hear My voice; and there will be one flock and one shepherd. (Jesus was speaking of the Gentiles.) Therefore My Father loves Me, because I lay down My life that I may take it again. No one takes it from Me, but I lay it down of Myself. I have power to lay it down, and I have power to take it again. This command I have received from My Father." Therefore there was a division again among the Jews because of these sayings. And many of them said, "He has a demon and is mad. Why do you listen to Him?" Others said, "These are not the words of one who has a demon. Can a demon open the eyes of the blind?"

> Now it was the Feast of Dedication in Jerusalem, and it was winter. And Jesus walked in the temple, in Solomon's porch. Then the Jews surrounded Him and said to Him, "How long do You keep us in doubt? If You are the Christ, tell us plainly." Jesus answered them, "I told you, and you do not believe. The works that I do in My Father's name, they bear witness of Me. But you do not believe, because you are not of My sheep, as I said to you. My sheep hear My voice, and I know them, and they follow Me. And I give them eternal life, and they shall never perish; neither shall anyone snatch them out of My hand. My Father, who has given *them* to Me, is greater than all; and no one is able to snatch *them* out of My Father's hand. I and *My* Father are one."

> —John 10:16-30

Jesus could not have told these "religious" leaders any more plainly Who He was, but they did not have ears to hear Him. He told them they were not His sheep, and they tried to stone Him. People who argue about the truth of the Scriptures, or whether God speaks to His people today, are like the Jewish leaders who accused and tried to stone Jesus. They don't have ears to hear because they have no revelation of Who Jesus is, and His Word is not alive in them. They can't hear what the Spirit is saying and it makes them angry. That is why controversy is stirred up when a true shepherd speaks the truth of God's Word, or shares what the Master has revealed to him by the Spirit.

Infiltrating The Enemy's Camp

Did you know that in addition to giving you ears to hear what His Spirit is saying God will reveal the enemy's plans to you? He will allow you to hear or see what is being plotted in the enemy's camp. This may sound far out, but God did it in the Bible. The Lord allowed Elisha to hear the battle plans the Syrian king spoke of in his bedroom so Elisha could warn the king of Israel. Let's read how this took place:

> Now the king of Syria was making war against Israel; and he consulted with his servants, saying, "My camp *will be* in such and such a place." And the man of God sent to the king of Israel, saying, "Beware that you do not pass this place,

> for the Syrians are coming down there." Then the king of Israel sent *someone* to the place of which the man of God had told him. Thus he warned him, and he was watchful there, not just once or twice. Therefore the heart of the king of Syria was greatly troubled by this thing; and he called his servants and said to them, "Will you not show me which of us *is* for the king of Israel?" And one of his servants said, "None, my lord, O king; but Elisha, the prophet who *is* in Israel, tells the king of Israel the words that you speak in your bedroom"
>
> —2 Kings 6:8-12

The king of Syria was so angry, he sent his army to go capture Elisha. When Elisha's servant went outside the next morning, he saw the army surrounding the city and was afraid. Here is Elisha's response to his servant:

> "Do not fear, for those who *are* with us *are* more than those who *are* with them." And Elisha prayed, and said, "LORD, I pray, open his eyes that he may see." Then the LORD opened the eyes of the young man, and he saw. And behold, the mountain *was* full of horses and chariots of fire all around Elisha.
>
> —2 Kings 6:16-17

Elisha's servant saw the army of Lord — legions of warring angels — ready to fight on Elisha's behalf. He was seeing in the spiritual realm.

It Still Happens Today

You may be saying, "But that was in Bible days. It can't happen like that today." I am here to tell you, it can and it does. The spiritual realm is as real as the natural realm. I'm not saying everyone can see and hear in the spiritual realm, but many do.

A young woman with a gift of discerning spirits was preparing to join her husband and his parents in an intercessory prayer session for their deliverance and inner-healing ministry. She had settled her children down for a nap and was putting on her makeup when she had a vision. She saw three demons sitting with a map in front of them, making plans to attack the ministry.

In her spirit she sensed an overwhelming knowing that they were looking for a weak spot by which to enter in and cause disruption and havoc. She shared this vision with her husband and the others who had gathered for prayer. The ministry was at a critical place and God was raising them up to a higher level of effectiveness and accountability. As one well-known evangelist says, "New levels, new devils." This woman's vision and ability to hear and see in the spiritual realm allowed the prayer team to infiltrate the enemy's camp and pray strategically and offensively. Battles are won by a strong offense.

Angels Are Real!

Cheryl Salem is also one of those people God has given eyes to see *and* ears to hear in both the physical and spiritual realms. Here is an excerpt from her book, *An Angel's Touch*, describing one such instance that took place at a large ministry conference:

> I felt that rush of excitement in my spirit as I looked up and saw the most beautiful entrance of two thousand or more angelic beings into the sanctuary! With bursts of light, they came through the walls and ceiling as if nothing was there to prevent their entrance. The upper half of the auditorium was completely crowded with angels! There were so many splendid angelic creatures that they looked like a sea of angels.
>
> They were warriors. Every one of them had something in their hands. Some had "hand-to-hand" combat weapons. They appeared to hold things like knives, swords, shields, and many other objects obviously used in battle, but I was unable to identify the weapons. I noticed that a few of the angels had no weapons but were holding in their hands musical instruments that looked like trumpets. They looked as if they were waiting for their signal to play.
>
> The angels were standing shoulder to shoulder, flanked like soldiers at attention, facing in toward the center of the sanctuary. All of a sudden, a group of about fifty would turn their backs to us and begin to fight an unseen adversary. The en-

emy from the outside seemed to be trying to enter the building, and it appeared to be the job of the angels to defend the premises and keep the demonic forces out. An angelic force of about fifty or so, swished out of the ceiling leaving the remains of colored light particles dissipating in the air. It was as if they had gained the advantage in the warfare, and in "hot pursuit" they pushed the demonic forces beyond the walls of the building....

I could hear the activity of the angelic realm, and it was a war going on right in the middle of the preaching! The clink of metal against metal as weapons struck one another reverberated throughout the recesses of my spirit's ears! There were definitely sounds of war in this place. They were not talking. They were not singing. They were not shouting. They were fighting. And yet, I had no fear. None at all! Somehow I knew the angels were well capable of handling this situation.[3]

Cheryl went on to describe the beautiful, majestic colors and physical stature of the angels she saw and heard. Read a brief portion of what she said:

I have tried to think of "human" words to describe them, and it has been difficult. Seeing into the supernatural realm is kind of like looking into a film negative. You can see everything, and yet you can see what's behind it also! I have finally resigned myself to the fact that trying to describe the supernatural dimension with natural words and descriptions is almost impossible to accomplish. Although I can give you an idea of what I

was seeing, it's still not even close to the magni-
tude of the spiritual realm of which I was privi-
leged to partake with my eyes and ears![4]

I believe we are living in a time when it is absolutely imperative to know the voice of the Lord. It is
a matter of life or death to hear and obey what the
Spirit of the Lord says to do. I don't say this to put
fear into anyone. I say this from the depths of my
being because I care about God's sheep. The spiritual realm is real and battles are won and lost in that
realm. God wants you to be on the offense, not the
defense.

You can hear four different voices: the voice of
God's Spirit, the voice of the devil, the voice of others around you, and your own voice. If you aren't
able to discern one voice from another, now is the
time to sharpen your hearing and tune in to God's
voice. We are going to learn how to do this in the
coming chapters.

Chapter 13

Tuning In To God's Voice

Cindy Jacobs, co-founder with her husband Michael of Generals of Intercession, knows how to tune in to God's voice. One time while leading worship at a church in Colorado Springs, she stopped in the middle of a song and said, "The Lord just spoke to me and told me there is a man here today with a very hardened heart toward God. The Lord wants you to soften your heart and make your peace with Him today." She waited a few moments to let the words sink in. Then she said, "God showed me you are a pilot of a small airplane, and the devil has scheduled you to die in an airplane crash tomorrow because of an undetected mechanical problem."[1]

She didn't know anyone in that church in such a situation, but she spoke out what she heard the Lord speak to her. After the service a man in his forties came up to her and said, "Mrs. Jacobs, you were speaking to me. I am a Vietnam veteran, and I have been angry with God and hardened my heart toward Him ever since the war. In fact, I don't even know what I am doing in this church tonight. I'm not a member and have never been here before. I just felt a strong urge to come here tonight. I am a pilot of a small plane, and I was going to be flying tomorrow."[2]

This man broke down and repented of his sins. He gave his life to Jesus that night. He then went and inspected his airplane and discovered a serious mechanical problem he would not have found during his ordinary preflight inspection. If he had taken off in that airplane, he would certainly have crashed. What the devil had scheduled for him was canceled by a word from the Lord, given through a woman who knew how to tune in to the voice of the Lord.

It is critical to hear the Lord's voice in three key areas: in your personal life, for ministering to others and for your family. Overcoming a crisis depends on having an ear to hear what the Spirit is saying as the woman in the following story learned.

Disgraced But Not Forgotten

It was the 1940s, and the nation was at war. Myra was a destitute, forty-year-old practical nurse who had taken a job providing home care to an elderly man. One night the man's alcoholic son came home drunk and raped Myra. Striped of her dignity, shamed and humiliated, she wept for days. Then as it happens in three out of every one hundred rape cases, Myra discovered she was pregnant.

Myra went to the doctor and told him she wanted to terminate the pregnancy. At that time abortions were not legal, and the doctor refused to help her because he didn't feel it was right. An unwed mother was shunned and treated with disgrace in those days, and she was already struggling to make ends meet financially. Alone, desperate and contemplating suicide, she cried out to God and said, "Lord, I'm carrying this child, and I don't know what to do." God spoke to her heart and told her she should have the baby, and it would help bring joy to the world. From that point on she had peace in her heart.[3]

Myra was convinced she was going to have a girl and had picked out the name, Joy. When the doctor told her it was a baby boy, she named him James after one of the apostles in the Bible. The road ahead for that little boy was not an easy one.

Myra knew she couldn't provide for this baby and placed him in the home of a pastor and his wife. Five years later she returned and took him away from the only home and parents he knew. The next ten years were filled with instability, loneliness and pain, living in foster homes intermittently, and bouncing from place to place with his mother. James was shy, unsociable and didn't like being around people.

During his early teenage years, for some unexplained reason, Myra married the father of her son who was still a hopeless alcoholic. Life had been bad but it got worse. One night fearing for his life, James held his father, who was in a drunken rage, at gunpoint and called the police. His father was sent to prison, and his mother's life was in turmoil. James returned to the pastor's home where he had spent the first five years of his life.

At a Sunday night evangelistic meeting, James heard a group of teens share testimonies about a loving Father who was always there for them and how Jesus helped them with their problems. This young man who had never had the approval of his earthly father walked down the aisle and into the arms of His loving heavenly Father. James said he heard the voice of the Father say, "I'm pleased, James. You've done well, son. I'm pleased."[4]

That night the heart of an evangelist was awakened in a teenager by the name of James Robison. He tuned in to the voice of God and walked into the destiny God had planned for him before he was even born. The man of God that James Robison became has brought joy to millions of people throughout the world, as his ministry, *Life Today,* feeds hungry souls both natural and spiritual food.

Seek Your Destiny

When we tune in to the voice of God, He helps us through crises and turning points when we need to make important decisions about our destiny.

In 1976 I was in the living room of my tiny little ghetto house. I had been holding Bible studies in my home, but I needed to know what God wanted me to do with my life. I thought I might be called to ministry, and that appealed to me. I loved studying and reading God's Word and helping and teaching people. But I had a good job that I loved, and everything was going along pretty well in my life. I wanted God to tell me whether I was to stay where I was and make a career of it, go into some other occupation, or if I was to go into ministry.

Ask Expecting An Answer

I was frustrated and didn't know what to do. I was praying and thumbing through the Bible when this Scripture caught my attention:

> If you want to know what God wants you to do, ask him, and he will gladly tell you, for he is always ready to give a bountiful supply of wisdom to all who ask him; he will not resent it. But when you ask him, be sure that you really expect him to tell you, for a doubtful mind will be

> as unsettled as a wave of the sea that is driven
> and tossed by the wind; and every decision you
> then make will be uncertain, as you turn first
> this way and then that. If you don't ask with
> faith, don't expect the Lord to give you any solid
> answer.
>
> —James 1:5-8 (TLB)

I said, "Okay, Lord, I'm going to pray until I hear from you. I want to know what *You* want me to do. I like to preach and teach Your Word, but I don't want to be involved in any kind of selfish ambition or presumption. I only want what You want."

Here's this single guy with evangelistic track racks hanging on the walls and prayer altars in the window, lying on the floor between the couch and the coffee table, praying and praying and praying. I got quiet before the Lord, and this is the first time I ever remember speaking a prophetic word. Something powerful bubbled up out of my inner most being, and I had to speak it out loud. The prophetic word God was speaking to me was this:

"David, my son, I've called you to speak My Word. Now speak it faithfully. The prophet that hath a dream let him tell his dream but you have My Word. Therefore, speak My Word faithfully. What is chaff to the wheat?" Those words came out of Jeremiah. God spoke it to me in an articulate way that made sense to me.

Since that day I have never doubted the anointing and calling of God on my life. I'm not saying I haven't had some discouraging days and wanted to become a manager at McDonalds, but I've never doubted the calling of God on my life. I also know I'm not a hireling because I've stuck it out through the good times and the bad times. Jesus said, "My sheep know My voice." I have followed His voice to do what He has called and anointed me to do.

Beware Of Presumption

When we are tuning in to God's voice, we must be careful of our own fleshly desires. Presumption can get us into dangerous waters even when what we are doing appears to be a good thing.

A couple that loved the Lord was nearing retirement age and decided they wanted to become missionaries. They didn't know where they should go so the husband got out a globe, spun it around and stuck his finger on it. It landed on a small island. They decided that was where they would go to be missionaries. They may have stopped to inquire of the Lord whether this was His will, but they didn't wait for His answer.

In the excitement of their decision, they moved ahead selling their home and furniture and getting their affairs in order. This tropical island seemed like a nice place to retire. They had to hire a puddle jumper plane to get to the island. Flying over the island in that junkie little plane, they looked down and saw smoke. What they didn't know was that a civil war was being fought on the island, and as their plane prepared for landing, it was shot out of the air.

As the plane was falling out of the sky this couple may have said, "Lord, are we in presumption?" The next words out of their mouths may have been, "Never mind, Lord. It doesn't matter. We're with You now!"[5] No one knows for sure what he or she said or thought in those final moments of life.

In these days in which we are living, it is truly a matter of life and death to be in the right place at the right time and to be away from the wrong place at the right time. Being in presumption about God's calling, or trying to satisfy your own desires as to how and where you will serve the Lord can place you in a minefield. To avoid disastrous or deadly mistakes, you must be led by the Spirit of God and be clearly tuned in to His voice.

A Word Of Knowledge

At times God speaks to us so we can minister encouragement to someone else. We can be used to help someone through a difficult situation or to bring them to repentance. This is called a word of knowledge, and it is something you have no way of knowing except that the Lord is revealing it to you. It is important to inquire of the Lord whether you are to share it with the individual or if you are simply to pray for that person.

Earlier in the book I shared with you how Dr. Jack Deere learned God still speaks to His people today. While Dr. Deere was still a professor at the theological seminary, one of his top students popped his head in the door of Dr. Deere's office to say hello. As they chatted, the word, pornography, kept coming up in Dr. Deere's spirit. He didn't know what to do, but he felt he was to confront this young man. It was a risk, but in a kind, gentle way he said, "Are you struggling with anything?"

"No, not at all, why do you ask?"

"On, no reason at all — anyway, what were you saying?"

God wouldn't let it go. As they continued to talk the word, "pornography," kept flashing in Dr. Deere's head like a neon sign. Again he asked Robert, "Are you sure you don't have any guilt you haven't been able to get rid of?"

"No, why do you keep asking me this?" This time he sounded offended.

Dr. Deere knew he had to press in and said, "Are you addicted to pornography? Before you say anything, let me tell you something. Since you have been sitting in my office, I think God has been telling me you are into pornography. If you are, I will never tell anyone your name, and I will not get you dismissed from seminary or your church because of this. And finally, I think the Lord has been telling me this because He wants to set you free. And He wants to start today."[6]

The young man broke down and confessed he had been into pornography and some other things since he was a young teenager. Since coming to know the Lord, he had battled with this evil power by himself and had been steadily losing ground. Dr. Deere laid hands on this young man and rebuked the power of the devil, commanding the spirits of lust and bondage to leave him in Jesus' name. That young man walked out of Dr. Deere's office a changed man, set free and on fire for the Lord.

The next time Dr. Deere saw this young man his whole countenance and everything about him was different. He hugged Dr. Deere and almost shouted, "I'm a new person! I'm a new person! Something left me; I feel lighter. I don't think I'll ever go back into that bondage again."[7] This young man was able to get a fresh start because Dr. Deere was tuned in to the voice of the Lord, and was obedient with what he heard.

Ponder It In Your Heart

If the Lord shares a word of knowledge with you about another person, ponder it carefully in your heart. Ask the Lord if you are to share it with the person or if you are simply to pray for restoration. If you are to share it with the individual, let the Lord put His words in your mouth. Be gentle and humble, not judgmental or critical. Whatever you do, never succumb to the temptation to share it with anyone else. God doesn't give you a word of knowledge to turn it into gossip. If He can't trust you to hold a word in confidence, He won't be able to use you in this manner again.

Children Need Guidance

If you are a parent, I encourage you to tune in to the voice of the Lord regarding what is happening in your children's lives. Our children are under tremendous pressure and temptation. They need our guidance and direction whether they think they do or not. It is your responsibility to listen to what the Spirit is telling you to protect them.

My daughter, Trina, gets freaked out sometimes when I confront her with what the Lord has shown me is going on in her life. She thinks it is spooky. I am so thankful God loves her enough to speak to her daddy. Many times I know exactly how to pray because I hear the voice of the Lord. Other times, I know it is time to say something. Parents and grandparents have tremendous influence over their children and grandchildren if they listen to the voice of the Spirit.

A Prayer Blessing

Grandpa Maxwell, an old Wesleyan preacher, prayed for his grandchildren. One day he pulled his twelve-year-old grandson aside and said, "I have something to tell you. I was praying, and God spoke to me and told me you are going to preach the Gospel."[8]

The next Sunday, this twelve-year-old was in Sunday school, and his teacher pulled him aside and said, "I've been praying for you lately, and I feel God has put a call on your life and you are going to preach the Gospel."[9]

This young man held those words in his heart. After graduation from high school, he heard the call from the Lord and began preparing for ministry. Dr. John Maxwell was a pastor for many years and has authored numerous best-selling books on leadership.

He is now training pastors and leaders around the world on a full-time basis.

Pray and seek the Lord for each of your children, and if you get a word, go ahead and speak that word of prophecy into his or her life. Lay hands on them and pray over them. The blessing by the patriarch of the family spoken of in the Old Testament was sought after and cherished. It is sorely missing in today's society. Our children need to hear blessings spoken over them by their parents and grandparents.

Danger Averted

Tuning in to the voice of the Spirit may protect your family from danger or harm. A young mother with a new baby was exhausted from what seemed like endless nights without sleep. She sank down on the bed one morning and drifted into sleep. She had a dream in which she saw her husband fall from a tall ladder at their church. He was seriously injured with a fractured back. The Lord told her to get up and go pray. She was so tired it took all of her strength to get up and go downstairs to tell her husband what she had dreamed. He was on his way out the door to go do some repairs at church. They prayed and he went on to church.

Later that day, he returned home and told her he was repairing some sheetrock on the ceiling of the baptistery. The tall ladder on which he was standing started to slide out from under him, but it suddenly caught on something and he regained his balance. When he looked down, his three-year-old son was directly in line with where the ladder would have landed if it kept falling. This young woman was tuned in to the voice of the Lord and obeyed when He told her to pray. It saved her husband and son from serious injury and possible death.

The voice of God's Spirit protects us and gives us power when we minister. It protects us, our family and others from evil, changing us into the glorious image of God's Son so we can reflect His glory in the earth. Are you tuned in to God's voice? Do you have your hearing receptors fine-tuned to hear what He is saying amidst all the busyness of life? Stay tuned in to God's station and increase your faith level.

Chapter 14

Faith Comes By Hearing

A missionary who was on furlough was speaking at church in Michigan, telling the story of his small field hospital in Africa. Every two weeks he had to take a two-day bicycle ride to the closest city to get money from the bank and buy medical supplies for the hospital. He always stopped halfway and camped out in the jungle overnight. One day on the second leg of his journey, not far from the city, he came upon a man who had been hurt in a fight. He stopped and cleaned the man's wounds, witnessing to him about Jesus as he patched him up. When he finished, the man got up and went on his way. The missionary continued on to the bank, picked up his medical supplies and began his long ride back to the hospital. Again he stopped to camp out in the jungle at the halfway point.

Two weeks later the missionary made another trip to the city. The man he had bandaged up and ministered to on his last trip approached him as he rode into town and asked to talk with him. He said, "We had been watching you for several months and knew your whole routine. We knew you went to the bank and bought medical supplies and then took money and drugs back to your hospital always camping in the jungle on your way back. On your last journey five friends and I were planning to kill you and steal your money and drugs. However, when we came to your camp, we saw twenty-six armed guards around your pup tent."

The missionary stopped him and said, "Oh, no, I can assure you I don't have twenty-six armed guards. I was there all by myself."

The man said, "You don't understand. All six of us counted them. There were twenty-six armed guards around your tent!"

The missionary decided these armed guards must have been angels and praised the Lord he was protected, which is what he shared with the people at the church in Michigan. As he came to this point in the story, a man in the congregation stood up and said, "Excuse me. Please forgive me for interrupting, but I must know what date that incident occurred." The missionary had noted it in his journal and was able to give him the exact date.

The man from the church said, "It was night in Africa, but it was afternoon here in Michigan. I was on the golf course with some friends. We were just ready to tee off on the eighth hole when the Spirit of the Lord stopped me and said to pray for this medical missionary. (He named the man who had just shared his story.) I stopped and prayed but sensed it was so urgent that we needed more prayer support. I called some of the guys from church and we met at church for a big prayer meeting that day. In fact, the guys are here that were in that prayer meeting that day. All of you who can verify that we were praying that very day stand up."

The missionary was stunned as he counted twenty-six men who had been praying for him in Michigan at the time he was camped out in the jungle. A golfer was tuned in to the voice of the Lord, and gathered twenty-six obedient men of faith to pray for a medical missionary halfway across the world.

Two Ways God Speaks

Before we proceed any further, I want to explain the difference between how God speaks to us through His written word *and* His spoken word. In the Greek language there are two words for "word." One is "logos" and the other is "rhema." "Logos" is the inspired, written word of God we find in the Bible. It is the general revealed will of God that cannot be changed. The Bible is our number one foundational truth. "Rhema" is the anointed, spoken word of God for a given situation.

Don't let this be confusing. Here is a good analogy to help you separate the two. The "logos," written word of God is a beautiful gift, like a shiny new car. But it is the "rhema" word that puts gas in the car to make it go. It is the Holy Spirit that gives life to the "logos" word and turns it into a "rhema" word, spoken to us for a specific situation. Remember, "logos" is the car and "rhema" is the gas. The car can't run without the gas. The "logos" word of God doesn't come to life until the anointing of the Holy Spirit provides the spark to start the ignition and turn it into "rhema."

The Spirit Gives Life

Have you ever heard someone say, "I try to read the Bible, but it is so dry and boring I just don't get anything out of it?" The reason it is boring is because they are reading the "logos" word, as it is stated clearly in this Scripture:

> who also made us sufficient as ministers of the new covenant, not of the letter but of the Spirit; for the letter kills, but the Spirit gives life.

—2 Corinthians 3:6

The "letter" referred to here is the "logos" word of God that has no life until the Spirit anoints it and breathes life into it, turning it into "rhema."

The Spirit Ignites Faith

Another key Scripture we must examine is this:

> So then, faith cometh by hearing, and hearing by the word of God.
>
> —Romans 10:17 (KJV)

It also refers to "rhema," the spoken Word of God. This means you can listen to a sermon filled with Scriptures, but if the Holy Spirit does not anoint the word being preached, it won't produce faith in your life. It is the anointing of a word spoken by the voice of the Holy Spirit that produces faith.

Will The Real God Please Stand Up?

So, "rhema" is the voice of God speaking to our hearts for a specific situation. This is a true testimony that was recorded by the World Prayer Center in Colorado Springs.

Omar, a young Muslim, was talking to a Christian worker who was telling him about Jesus. Omar was reading the Koran but he was confused by so many different religions, each claiming to be the right one. The Christian worker said to Omar, "Why don't you go home and pray to Allah in the name of

175

Mohammed and see if Allah answers you. Pray in the name of Buddha and see if he answers you. Pray in the name of the Hindu gods and see if the god's answer you. Then pray to God in the name of Jesus. Whichever one gives you an answer to your prayer, believe that one."

It took a lot of faith for this Christian worker to tell Omar to do that. It was like saying, "Will the *real* God please stand up?" The Christian worker bound the devil so he couldn't interfere.

Omar went home and prayed, "Allah, you know I have a seeking heart. I really want to know the true and living God. I come to you in the name of Mohammed and ask you to speak to me." He waited ten minutes, twenty minutes and nothing happened.

"God, I come to you in the name of all the Hindu gods. I want you to speak to me. If you speak to me, I will worship all the Hindu gods." Again he waited and nothing happened.

"I come to you in the name of Buddha. I ask you to speak to me about the true way of peace. If you speak to me I will worship Buddha." He waited and waited but received no response.

Finally, he said, "God, I come to you in the name of Jesus that the missionary told me about. I ask you to speak to me. For you know I have a seeking, searching heart and want to know the true way." He no sooner finished his sentence than a voice said, "I love you, Omar. I am the Lord Jesus." Omar jumped up and said, "You are my Lord from this day forward. I will believe you and I will serve you all the days of my life."

Omar heard the anointed, spoken word of the Lord and it ignited his faith. He ran and told the Christian worker what had happened, was baptized and is serving the Lord today.

Can Mommy See Me?

Keith Hulen is the Director of Praise and Worship at Christ for the Nations Institute in Dallas, Texas. In November of 1999, Keith's beautiful, young wife, Kerri, went home to be with the Lord after battling with breast cancer. The following is an excerpt from Keith's testimony. It shows that the "rhema" word of God spoken through another person can ignite faith, even in a grieving child.

> When Kerri passed on, my thoughts turned toward my two small children, Dutch (7 years) and Taylor (5 years). How would they cope with this tremendous loss? It didn't take long for God to reveal Himself.
>
> Before Kerri's memorial service, I arrived early to make sure the casket and flowers were positioned correctly. I met my secretary in the sanctu-

ary where she handed me a note from a Christ for the Nations' student who felt it was a word from the Lord for me. I glanced at the note but became distracted by other things. After meeting briefly with the funeral director, I went into the speaker's chamber in the prayer room. I once again glanced at the note. It didn't make sense to me, so I simply laid it on the end table. Pastor Randy arrived and we began to discuss the service. We then left the room to pray with the family and begin the service. The note remained in the prayer room.

In the middle of the service, my son, Dutch, needed to use the rest room. My mother took him. When he was finished, he didn't want to go back into the service, so they went into the prayer room. He began to open up and express his feelings. "Nanna," he said, "I wish I had a telephone that could reach all the way to Heaven so I could talk to Mommy. I miss her so much. I know that now I have to speak to her in my heart, but I need to know, can my Mommy see me? And does she know where I am and how I feel?"

The question was loaded. My mother began to try to answer. As they sat down in the speaker's chamber, Dutch's eyes fell upon the note sitting on the end table and noticed his mother's name had been written on it. He picked up the note and said, "Nanna, would you read me this note that has Mommy's name on it?" The note said, "Kerri wants you to know that the answer to your question is, 'Yes.' She can see you. Tell her son that she loves him very much!"

Dutch's eyes lit up as he embraced the message in the note. His Mommy could see him and did love him! It was a defining moment for Dutch and something I will never forget…The gift of God was activated in someone's heart and used by the Holy Spirit to communicate God's heart to a seven-year-old boy who had just lost his mother. He reigns magnificently![1]

Put The Devil On The Run

The "rhema" word is needed to defeat the devil. Reference made to the sword of the spirit in the armor of God in Ephesians 6:17 refers to "rhema" word. You can hold up a Bible to the devil and shake it in his face all day long, and he won't do anything but laugh. When the devil came to tempt Jesus in the wilderness, Jesus didn't hold up the Old Testament scrolls to him, He *spoke* the "rhema" word and the devil left. To conquer the devil you must speak "rhema" word to him.

The golfer in the story you read earlier heard a "rhema" word from the Lord, and it stirred the faith of twenty-six men to do battle in the heavenlies for a missionary's protection. The men in the jungle who came to kill the missionary saw the spirits of these twenty-six prayer warriors praying the "rhema" word, forming a hedge of protection around that missionary's camp.

There are two realms: the natural and the spiritual. The robbers thought those guards looked pretty intimidating. God lifted the veil of the spiritual realm and let them see the spiritual prayer warriors who were protecting the missionary. That's how powerful the "rhema" word of God is. Never underestimate how critical your prayers are on behalf of those people God puts on your heart to pray for. The army we have in the spiritual realm, whether prayer warriors or angels, is bigger than any army that could ever be against us.

Take comfort and courage in knowing in that invisible, spiritual realm ,there is a God who loves you enough to speak to you about important things in your life and to dispatch His army on your behalf. Sometimes He speaks by anointing His written word, making it rhema; sometimes by speaking directly to your spirit, and sometimes by using other revelatory gifts such as dreams in the night season.

Chapter 15

Dreams In The Night Season

Evangelist James Robison had a dream one night about having a fatal car accident at a dangerous highway intersection. He and his family prayed for his protection because he travels often.

Not long after that, James came to that exact intersection. A van was alongside of him in the left lane, and he was getting ready to accelerate to move out onto the highway when suddenly he saw the dream unfolding in front of his eyes. He hit the brakes just as a sports car came out of nowhere in the lane he would have pulled into if he hadn't braked. The sports car sped by, cutting off the van. There was no doubt it would have smashed into James' car if he had pulled into that lane. The memory of the dream saved his life.

A few weeks later James shared that dream at a conference and how his life had been spared because of the warning. After the conference, James and one of the elders from the church went golfing. The elder was driving and had a green light as he approached a certain intersection. The dream James had described the day before flashed in the man's memory and he slowed down. At that moment a car pulled right into the intersection ahead of them. The man with whom James was riding slammed on his brakes. The two cars collided, but because James' car had slowed down there was little damage and no one was injured.

The man said to James, "If I hadn't been thinking about the dream, I would have never seen the other car pulling out in front of us." God only knows how tragic a wreck could have happened.[1]

James' dream saved his life, not once but twice. God often uses dreams to warn of danger.

It is extremely rare to hear a teaching from the pulpit on dreams or visions. Yet, in studying the Bible, dreams and visions were a common occurrence. In an earlier chapter we read the Scripture in Acts 2:17 where Peter was quoting the prophet Joel. Peter only changed one word. Peter replaced "afterward" with "in the last days." Dreams, visions and prophecy are revelatory gifts that Peter was saying were to be signs of the last days:

And it shall come to pass *in the last days*, saith God, I will pour out of my Spirit upon all flesh; and your sons and your daughters shall prophesy, and your young men shall see visions, and your old men shall dream dreams.

— Acts 2:17 (KJV)

And it shall come to pass *afterward, that* I will pour out my Spirit upon all flesh; and your sons and your daughters shall prophesy, your old men shall dream dreams, your young men shall see visions.

—Joel 2:28 (KJV)

Is It A Dream Or A Vision?

When we talk about dreams, we are talking about those things that happen in the night season while we sleep. We aren't talking about the kind of dreams or desires you might have to build a house or to be a concert pianist. Dreams occur when you are sleeping with your eyes closed. A vision is when you see something with your mind's eye, while you are wide-awake. In 2 Kings 6:17 when Elisha's servant looked out and saw God's army of angels sent to protect them from the Syrian king's army, he was having a vision. When Jack Deere saw the word "pornography" flashing before his eyes while talking to the seminary student, he was having a vision. Primarily I want to talk about dreams in this chapter.

Throughout history God has spoken through dreams and visions. We can read various accounts of this from Genesis through Revelation. In fact, the entire book of Revelation is actually a dream God gave to the apostle John.

Joseph – The Dreamer

In the Old Testament Joseph is one of the most memorable dreamers. If you want to read his story, it begins in Genesis 37. When Joseph was seventeen years old, he had two dreams that showed his brothers and parents bowing down to him. In his immaturity he shared the dreams with his brothers, who hated him for it. His father also rebuked him, but thought about what Joseph had said and wondered what it meant.

Joseph's brothers became so jealous of him they sold him as a slave, and Joseph ended up in Egypt. He continued to be a dreamer and was able to interpret dreams for others. By the Lord's grace he was placed in positions of responsibility and shown favor wherever he was: first in Potiphar's house, then in prison and finally as second-in-command in Pharaoh's kingdom. Years later, his early dreams came true when his brothers came to Egypt in search of food. They didn't recognize Joseph, who was the governor over the land, when they bowed before him as we can read here:

> Now Joseph was the governor of the land, the one who sold grain to all its people. So when Joseph's brothers arrived, they bowed down to him with their faces to the ground.
>
> — Genesis 42:6 (NIV)

Joseph was able to save the lives of his father, mother and brothers during the famine. God used Joseph to protect the lineage of Abraham, Jacob and Isaac, which included future kings and priests such as King David and eventually Jesus Christ, our King and High Priest.

Another Joseph Dreams

In the first two chapters of the New Testament we read of God speaking to another Joseph, Jesus' stepfather, in dreams:

> This is how the birth of Jesus Christ came about: His mother Mary was pledged to be married to Joseph, but before they came together, she was found to be with child through the Holy Spirit. Because Joseph her husband was a righteous man and did not want to expose her to public disgrace, he had in mind to divorce her quietly. But after he had considered this, an angel of the Lord appeared to him in a dream and said, "Joseph son of David, do not be afraid to take Mary home as your wife, because what is conceived in her is from the Holy Spirit. She will give birth

to a son, and you are to give him the name Jesus, because he will save his people from their sins."

— Matthew 1:18-21 (NIV)

When they had gone, an angel of the Lord appeared to Joseph in a dream. "Get up," he said, "take the child and his mother and escape to Egypt. Stay there until I tell you, for Herod is going to search for the child to kill him." So he got up, took the child and his mother during the night and left for Egypt, where he stayed until the death of Herod. And so was fulfilled what the Lord had said through the prophet: "Out of Egypt I called my son."

—Matthew 2:13-15 (NIV)

After Herod died, an angel of the Lord appeared in a dream to Joseph in Egypt and said, "Get up, take the child and his mother and go to the land of Israel, for those who were trying to take the child's life are dead." So he got up, took the child and his mother and went to the land of Israel. But when he heard that Archelaus was reigning in Judea in place of his father Herod, he was afraid to go there. Having been warned in a dream, he withdrew to the district of Galilee, and he went and lived in a town called Nazareth. So was fulfilled what was said through the prophets: "He will be called a Nazarene."

—Matthew 2:19-23 (NIV)

God preserved the life of His Son, Jesus, by warning His stepfather in dreams to keep Him out of Herod's grasp. Joseph was a man of integrity and obeyed the voice of the Lord each time. He didn't stop and say, "Oh, that must have been the pizza I ate last night," or, "That sure was a crazy, mixed up dream. My imagination must be playing tricks on me!" Joseph recognized God's voice and honored His authority even when it meant people might criticize and scoff at him for marrying a woman who was already pregnant.

Dreams Have Gotten A Bad Rap

It is quite unusual to find a solid Christian today who pays any attention to dreams, because dreams are regarded as psychological, emotional, stress-related activities of the mind during sleep. This skepticism is largely due to the twisted, false writings of Carl Jung and Sigmund Freud. Some psychologists say dreams are just a reaction of the nervous system to physical stimuli, or a rehashing of yesterday's experiences. Others say dreams are meaningless, inconsequential occurrences. Then there are those who say dreams are from the occult and are just the devil's way of unlocking the hidden secrets of the spirit world. [2]

Don't Turn Off The Channel

I am one of the first to admit that some dreams are senseless and should be disregarded. However, I don't believe we should throw the baby out with the bath water just because the secular teaching about dreams is false or misleading. Some dreams come from God, and if we don't believe it, we may be turning off the very channel on which God is trying to broadcast an important message or warning.

Many contemporary experiences are recorded of God's people having world-changing dreams. Bill Bright, founder of Campus Crusade for Christ, had a dream about reaching the world for Christ and built a powerful ministry. What if he hadn't believed the dream was from God and ignored what God was showing him to do? How many college students might never have heard the message of the Gospel?

A woman attended a Benny Thomas meeting and heard him teach about God speaking through dreams. She went home that night and prayed that God would give her a dream to help her son. She dreamed about her teenage son who was having some serious behavioral and disciplinary problems. In that dream she was given clear instructions on how to discipline her son and correct his behavioral problems. When she awoke the next morning, she said, "Lord, was that dream from You?" A peace settled in her heart, and she wrote down the detailed instructions she had received in the dream. As she applied these instructions and changed the way she was dealing with her son, his behavior problems were corrected, and there was peace in their home.

Believe And Ask For Dreams

God can give you dreams about your business, your schoolwork, your family or any other area of life. However, He doesn't seem to give dreams to those who don't believe He speaks in dreams, and often He doesn't give dreams to those who don't bother to ask Him for dreams.

God works in partnership with us here on earth. He has chosen to work through prayer, but it must be guided. Many times I have dreamed about individuals in our church, and I knew it was a message from God for me to pray in a specific way for these people. Prayer must be like a guided missile, not like a shotgun. It must be focused and specific. That is why God often gives us specific instructions in our dreams.

Faith is only activated by something specific. General prayers that say, "God bless me or God help me" are not targeted enough to receive an answer. Dr. David Yonggi Cho, pastor of the largest church in the world in Seoul, Korea tells a story about the early days of his ministry when he asked the Lord for a desk, a chair and a bicycle. He believed and praised the Lord but month after month passed with no answer to his prayer. The work he was doing was very hard, and one day he cried out to the Lord. Here is an excerpt from his book, *The Fourth Dimension:*

Lord, I asked you to supply me with a desk, a chair and a bicycle several months ago, but you have not supplied me with any of those things. Now you see me as I am here preaching the Gospel to the poverty stricken people of this slum area. How can I ask them to exercise faith when I cannot even practice it myself? How can I ask them to put their faith in the Lord, and truly live by the Word, and not by bread?

My Father! I am very discouraged. I am not sure about this, but I do know I cannot deny the Word of God. The Word must stand, and I am sure that you are going to answer me, but this time I'm just not sure when or how. If you are going to answer my prayer after my death, what kind of profit will that have for me? If you are ever going to answer my prayer, please speed it up. Please!

Then I sat down and began to cry. Suddenly I felt a serenity, and a feeling of tranquility came into my soul. Whenever I have that kind of feeling, a sense of the presence of God, He always speaks; so I waited. Then that still, small voice welled up in my soul, and the Spirit said, "My son, I heard your prayer a long time ago."

Right away I blurted out, "Then where are my desk, chair and bicycle?"

The Spirit said, "Yes, that is the trouble with you, and with all my children. They beg me, demanding every kind of request, but they ask in such vague terms that I can't answer. Don't you know there are dozens of kinds of desks, chairs

and bicycles? But you've simply asked me for a desk, chair and bicycle. You never ordered a specific desk, chair or bicycle."

That was a turning point in my life. No professor in Bible College ever taught me along these lines. I had made a mistake, and it was an eye-opener for me.

I then said, "Lord, do you really want me to pray in definite terms?" This time the Lord led me to turn to Hebrews, the eleventh chapter: "Faith is the substance of things, (clear cut things) hoped for."[3]

Dr. Cho repented of his mistake and changed the way he prayed. He got specific about the desk, chair and bicycle, and here is what he said,

I was praising the Lord, and sure enough, when the time came, I had every one of those things. I had exactly all the things I had asked for — a desk made out of Philippine mahogany; a chair made by the Japanese Mitsubishi Company, with rollers on the tips so that I could roll around when I sat on it; and a slightly used bicycle, with gears on the side, from an American missionary's son. I brought that desk, chair and bicycle into my house and was completely changed in my prayer attitude.

Until that time I had always prayed in vague terms, but from that time until now I have never prayed in vague terms. If God were ever to answer your vague prayers, then you would never recog-

nize that prayer as being answered by God. You
must ask definitely and specifically.[4]

I hope Dr. Cho's story is as much of an eye-opener
for you about your prayer attitude as it was for him.
Faith goes after something specific. As you pray a
specifically targeted prayer, God will hear and answer your prayer, and there will be no question it
came from him.

The woman who attended Benny Thomas' meeting prayed specifically for a dream to help her son,
and God gave her a dream that instructed her how to
help him. She knew she had heard from God when
she saw the changes taking place in her son.

God will speak to you in dreams if you believe
He will and if you ask Him for dreams. Often God
warns us of danger in dreams and gives us specific
instructions how to pray. In the coming chapter we
are going to discuss five reasons God gives people
dreams.

Chapter 16

Why God Speaks In Dreams

In a Muslim village a group of men studying the Koran noticed a man named Jesus was mentioned more often than Mohammed. They began to ask, "Who is this man Jesus the Koran is talking about?" The leader of the study group went home that night, fell asleep and had a dream. In his dream a big man came to him and said, "You have wondered who the Man Jesus is. Tomorrow at ten o'clock on such and such bridge, some people will be there to introduce you to this Man Jesus about whom you have been reading. They will give you literature to bring back to your village for everyone else to know Jesus."

In the morning when the man woke up, the dream was still vivid in his mind. He gave himself plenty of time to get to the bridge.

Meanwhile, a missionary couple was leaving a village with Bibles, Christian literature and tracts in their jeep. They were disappointed that no one in this village had wanted to hear about Jesus. They wouldn't even accept any of their literature. The couple decided to drive on to the next town. Coming to a bridge outside the town to which they were driving, the engine on their jeep died right in the middle of the bridge. They tried and tried to start it, but it just wouldn't turn over. Everything under the hood looked all right, but it wouldn't start.

They noticed a man running down a hill towards them. He came right up to them on the bridge and said, "Hello. I'm here to be introduced to the Man Jesus!"

The missionaries looked at him in surprise and said, "Who sent you here?"

He said, "Last night I had a dream. A big man told me to come to this bridge at ten o'clock this morning and someone would introduce me to Jesus and give me literature to take to my people to introduce them to Jesus."

The missionaries led this man to Jesus right there on the bridge, loaded him up with a knapsack and bags full of literature and Bibles, and sent him on his way. He was all smiles as he hurried back toward his village with his special cargo.

The missionaries watched him climb back up the hillside he had run down and disappear out of sight. When the missionary turned the key in the ignition of the jeep, it started right up, and they drove on to the next town.[1]

God still speaks to people through dreams because He loves and cares for every person on this earth. If a dream is the only way to tell someone about His love, then that is the avenue of communication He will use. Let's explore five reasons why God speaks in dreams.

Reason Number 1: To answer specific questions.

The Bible holds the answers to all truth, but sometimes we need answers to some very specific questions that apply to the practical aspects of every day life. Here is an example:

A pastor who had written a book needed to do the final edit on his manuscript before sending it to the publisher the following week. When he arrived at home and opened his briefcase, he was shocked to discover the manuscript was missing. He called his office and had his assistant search his office, but the manuscript was not there. He went out and searched his car thinking perhaps it had slid under the seat or something, but the manuscript was nowhere to be found. He remembered working on it at the office and carrying it out to the car so he could work on it at home that evening.

To say he was upset was an understatement. There was no duplicate copy because he had thrown the previous drafts away so he wouldn't mix them up with the final draft. All of his notes, which had taken considerable time, were written on the final draft copy. The publisher was expecting the final draft no later than next week so the production schedule would not be delayed. The press time was already reserved and missing the deadline would be disastrous. What was he going to do?

Before he went to bed that night, the pastor prayed, "God, I don't know where that manuscript is, but You do. I just ask You to show me where it is."

He fell asleep and had a dream that he was driving down the road he usually took to drive between home and the office. He saw a package on the side of the road. He stopped the car, got out and picked up the package. At that moment the dream ended and he woke up. The dream was so vivid he got out of bed, put on his clothes, got in his car and drove slowly along the road he saw in his dream. His headlights flashed on a package beside the road right where it had been in his dream. He stopped and picked up the brown envelope that held his manuscript.

Then he remembered what he had done. As he was loading things into the car that afternoon, he had set the manuscript on the roof of the car but never put it inside. As he drove off, the manuscript rode on the roof of the car for quite a long way before it finally tumbled off onto the side of the road.[2] God knew where it was and answered this man's prayer through a dream. What if he hadn't believed God still speaks in dreams and had just turned over and gone back to sleep? God will answer your questions if you ask Him.

Reason Number 2: To lead people to Christ.

The only way to God, the Father, is through Jesus Christ, His Son. Jesus was conceived by the Holy Spirit and born of the virgin, Mary. He led a sinless life and died on the cross for our sins, not His sins. Then He was raised from the dead and ascended into Heaven. He is the only Mediator between God and man. Nobody can get to Heaven any other way but by coming through Jesus Christ. They must turn from sin and turn to Christ, publicly confessing Jesus as Lord. It is the only way to eternal life.

We all know people who are religious. Jesus met many in His day as well. However, it isn't good enough to just be religious. A person must have a personal relationship with Jesus Christ to make it into Heaven.

God is so crazy in love with people that He will sometimes give an unsaved person a dream that will lead them to someone or some place that they can hear the message of Christ and be saved. We read about how this can happen in the story at the beginning of this chapter. According to Carl Menderas, a missionary in a Muslim country, that story is not unique. God often gives Muslims dreams about Jesus. When they come to try to find out Who Jesus is, God has already prepared their hearts.

We have to remember it is up to man to preach the Gospel. Even angels can't preach the Gospel. It is up to man. So God will lead people through dreams to a place where they can hear the Gospel. It is part of His plan.

At one of Carl's meetings, a Muslim man briefly listened to what Carl was preaching and fell to his knees, crying that Jesus had saved him. Then he went on to explain. A week earlier this Muslim man had a dream in which he was bound like a mummy in chains. He was in a deep pit with no way to get out. It was hopeless. Then a Man reached down His hand, pulled him out of the pit, broke the chains off of him and set him free.

Then this Muslim man heard Carl Menderas say, "Jesus Christ will lift you out of the deep pit of sin and despair. He will break the chains off your life and set you free." In that instant the dream flashed back across the man's mind and he knew what the dream meant. Jesus had been the Man who had saved him.[3]

Other times God may give a Christian a dream to show them specifically how to reach someone who isn't saved, as He did in this story.

A young evangelist just out of seminary had a heart for God. He was preaching at a church and heard about a man whose wife had died and left him with two daughters. The wife had prayed her husband would be saved before she died, but it didn't happen. The pastors at the church had tried to witness to him but were unable to touch his heart. Once in a while he came to church with his daughters, but nothing seemed to move him. He was totally cold to the Gospel. He was a good man and a moral man that loved and cared deeply for his family. After hearing this story from the man's two daughters, the evangelist prayed and said, "God, help me to reach this man. I don't know how to do it, but I want to touch his life and lead him to Christ."

That night the evangelist had a dream. He was at this man's house sitting in the living room. The man said, "Can I get you anything?"

"Just a cup of water would be fine."

"I'll go out and get you one."

As he walked out to the kitchen, the evangelist followed him and said, "You have two of the most beautiful daughters in the whole world."

"I sure do and I love 'em."

"I know you would do anything for those two daughters, wouldn't you?"

"I'd do anything for them. I love 'em. I'm so proud of them."

In his dream the evangelist looked at the man and said, "It's too bad you can't give them the one thing they need the most."

The man looked at him rather surprised and said, "What's that?"

"A Christian father." The evangelist woke up from his dream.

The next day after preaching a service, the evangelist decided to go visit the man he had dreamed about. The man invited him and they sat in the living room chatting. The man said, "Can I get you anything?" The conversation and events continued to play out exactly as it had been in the evangelist's dream.

When the evangelist said, "A Christian father," the man burst into tears. The Holy Spirit hit him and penetrated his soul that night, and the man said, "Pray for me. I want to know Jesus as my Savior. I want to be the Christian father I should be for those girls." Right there in the kitchen, that evangelist led this man to the Lord. It all happened because of a dream.[4]

If you have unsaved loved ones, pray and ask God to begin to give them dreams that will cause them to be troubled in their spirit until they come seeking the answer – Jesus Christ. Ask God to give you a dream to show you specifically how to share the answer with them.

Reason Number 3: To give instructions.

We touched on this in the last chapter. Jesus' stepfather, Joseph, followed God's instructions given to him in dreams to protect baby Jesus from King Herod. A woman received instructions how to discipline her son and correct his bad behavior through a dream.

It is clearly evident that God sends dreams to instruct and give us guidance. In Matthew we read of

Pontius Pilate's wife having a dream and telling her husband not to harm Jesus. She said:

> While Pilate was sitting on the judge's seat, his wife sent him this message: "Don't have anything to do with that innocent man, for I have suffered a great deal today in a dream because of him."
>
> — Matthew 27:19 (NIV)

Pilate didn't listen to his wife's message. He was a crowd pleaser and listened as they cried, "Crucify Him!" He tried to pass the blame off on the Jewish leaders and the crowd, but Pilate has gone down in history as the one that ordered the execution of the very Son of God. You sure don't hear of people naming their kids Pontius Pilate anymore!

Sometimes when a situation seems to be impossible and you don't know what to do, God will give you a dream to guide you to the right solution. Read how He did just that for this pastor.

The pastor was having trouble in his church. The members were bickering and fighting among themselves. There was rivalry, jealousy and envy, and it was tearing the congregation apart. The pastor tried everything he knew to bring unity but nothing worked. He went home one night and prayed, "God, what am I to do with these people? There are so many schisms the church is becoming more divided by the day. I just don't know what to do."

He fell asleep and had a dream that he went to the church and all he found was a pile of ashes smoldering on the ground. The church had burned to the ground. He saw the members standing around the ashes and heard them murmuring. One group said, "I'll bet the Jones' did this." The other group said, "You know the Smiths did this." They were pointing fingers and blaming each other.

The pastor then heard hideous laughter off in the distance. He looked over, and there was the devil laughing up a storm. Satan was laughing so hard he was rolling on the ground because he had everyone fighting against each other. With an evil look in his eye and a hideous smile on his face, the devil looked at the pastor and said, "I did it!" It was so bone chilling the pastor woke up with a start.

The next Sunday the pastor got up in the pulpit and said, "Ladies and gentlemen, I had a dream I want to share with you." He told them about the smoldering ash and how everyone was blaming one another. When he told them what the devil said, there was total silence in the sanctuary.

Do you know what happened? The Holy Spirit fell on the congregation and people began repenting of their jealousy, bickering and backbiting. They identified whom their real enemy was — the devil — and realized they didn't want their church destroyed. As repentance flowed, families and friends came together. There was unity in the congregation and revival came to that church.

If you are struggling in some area of your life or facing difficult circumstances, pray and ask the Lord to give you instruction and guidance about what to do. As you submit to Him, an answer will come.

Reason Number 4: To give you intercessory guidance how to pray specifically for others.

Have you ever had a bad dream about someone you love and didn't know what to do about it? If that happens, don't just pass it off as a scary nightmare. Pray and ask the Lord what it means and how you should pray for that person. The Lord may be giving you forewarning of something so you can pray.

Cindy Johnson was a senior in high school when she had a terrible dream that her daddy had died. She had been with him in the living room of her home and he looked gray and colorless. Alarmed at how bad he looked, she said, "Daddy, are you okay? Are you feeling all right?" Her dad just looked up at her and said, "Oh, darling, I'm just very tired."

When Cindy woke up, she ran to her daddy's room to see if he was alive. He was fine, and she was relieved it was just a nightmare. She simply forgot about the dream.

A few years later Cindy came home from college to visit her dad. She found him in the living room wrapped in a blanket just like she had seen in her dream. His skin was pale and colorless. She walked over to him and said, "Daddy, are you okay? Are you feeling all right?" Her dad looked up at her and said, "Oh, darling, I'm just very tired." Three months later Cindy's father had a massive heart attack and died at the age of 49. She was devastated.[5]

Cindy, who is now Cindy Jacobs, did not know she was called to be a prophetic intercessor or that she would have a worldwide prayer ministry. At the time she had the dream about her father and even at the time of his death, she knew nothing about prophetic dreams or intercessory prayer. Her dad knew the Lord, but he needed someone to stand in the gap for him and do warfare against the enemy who comes to steal, kill and destroy, as it says in this Scripture:

> **The thief comes only to steal and kill and destroy; I have come that they may have life, and have it to the full.**
>
> **—John 10:10 (NIV)**

We all need someone to stand in the gap for us. That is why I so appreciate my 120 prayer partners that pray for my family and me every day. I praise God that if He gives them a dream or tells them something about me, it is so they can pray it through on my behalf, like what happened in this next story.

Stella had never been taught about dreams in her church, but she was a strong Christian. One night Stella had a dream about a dear friend named Mrs. Simpson. In the dream she saw Mrs. Simpson walking with her hands over her head acting absolutely insane. The dream was so real, Stella called her friend, shared the dream with her and said, "Please go to the doctor and have a check up."

Mrs. Simpson said, "I feel better than I've ever felt in my life." Because of her love for her friend and because of the urgency she felt about the dream, Stella persisted and convinced Mrs. Simpson to go see her doctor. She was shocked when the doctor discovered a tumor in a portion of the brain that if it grew, it would take away her sanity.

Her doctor sent her to Mayo Clinic in Minneapolis. Dr. Will Mayo was still practicing at that time and he said to Mrs. Simpson, "Let's wait for three months, live healthily and apply all the faith you have."[6]

Mrs. Simpson went to a cabin in the woods and got close to God. She started reading all the healing Scriptures and talking to God. She thanked God for giving Stella the dream and for caring enough to convince her to go to the doctor. She prayed and prayed and prayed, getting to know God more intimately, and to know more about His creative miracles, His loving kindness and His mercy. When she went back to see Dr. Mayo three months later, the tumor was gone. God gave her a miracle.

If Stella hadn't had the dream and urged her friend to go to the doctor, there was no way she would have known how to pray specifically for her healing or for others to pray on her behalf. As we've already discussed, prayer must be targeted like a guided missile. If you are at war out in the middle of the ocean, you don't just start shooting torpedoes anywhere and everywhere hoping to the hit the enemy ship. You find out where the enemy ship is and then you shoot the torpedo or missile at the target. Targeted prayer is what produces miracles, which is one reason God gives us prophetic dreams.

Reason Number 5: To warn us of unseen dangers and to provide an opportunity for repentance.

We have already talked of several instances in which dreams provided a warning to save lives. In the last chapter James Robison's dream saved his life twice. The story we just read about Mrs. Simpson is another example. Without Stella's dream, there would have been no warning of the dangerous tumor growing in Mrs. Simpson's brain. Here is another example:

Jack Taylor, a powerful man of God, was growing sicker and sicker from an unknown ailment. Medical specialists could not diagnose the problem. He was only fifty years old but he was getting weaker and weaker.

One night an angel came to him in a dream and said, "Jack, the medicine you are taking is killing you." The angel named the specific medicine. Jack was taking four or five different medicines at the time trying to treat the symptoms.

Upon awaking from the dream, Jack got up, went to the medicine cabinet and looked through the prescriptions he was taking. He found the one the angel had named and set it aside. The next day he went to his doctor and asked him to look up the side effects of that particular medicine. The doctor reviewed all of the medications Jack was taking and discovered the medicine the angel had warned about was not compatible with one of the other medications. It was causing his kidneys to shut down and could have been fatal if he had continued to take it. Jack's life was spared because of a dream.[7]

In Scripture we find numerous examples of warnings given in dreams. The prophet Daniel dreamed dreams and also interpreted dreams. He interpreted dreams for King Nebuchadnezzar, including the one that foretold the loss of his kingdom in the fourth chapter of Daniel. Here is the warning Daniel gave the king:

> This is the interpretation, O king, and this is the decree the Most High has issued against my lord the king: You will be driven away from people and will live with the wild animals; you will eat grass like cattle and be drenched with the dew of heaven. Seven times will pass by for you until you acknowledge that the Most High is sovereign over the kingdoms of men and gives them to anyone he wishes. The command to leave the stump of the tree with its roots means that your kingdom will be restored to you when you acknowledge that heaven rules. Therefore, O king, be pleased to accept my advice: Renounce your sins by doing what is right, and your wickedness by being kind to the oppressed. It may be that then your prosperity will continue.
>
> —Daniel 4:24-27 (NIV)

Here is the account of the fulfillment of what was prophesied in the king's dream. It came about exactly as Daniel interpreted because the king did not heed the warning:

> All this happened to King Nebuchadnezzar. Twelve months later, as the king was walking on the roof of the royal palace of Babylon, he said, "Is not this the great Babylon I have built as the royal residence, by my mighty power and for the glory of my majesty?"
>
> The words were still on his lips when a voice came from heaven, "This is what is decreed for you, King Nebuchadnezzar: Your royal authority has been taken from you. You will be driven away from people and will live with the wild animals; you will eat grass like cattle. Seven times will pass by for you until you acknowledge that the Most High is sovereign over the kingdoms of men and gives them to anyone he wishes."
>
> Immediately what had been said about Nebuchadnezzar was fulfilled. He was driven away from people and ate grass like cattle. His body was drenched with the dew of heaven until his hair grew like the feathers of an eagle and his nails like the claws of a bird.
>
> At the end of that time, I, Nebuchadnezzar, raised my eyes toward heaven, and my sanity was restored. Then I praised the Most High; I honored and glorified him who lives forever.
>
> —Daniel 4:28-34a (NIV)

When a warning is given, be assured what is prophesied will take place if we don't heed the warning. The king could have avoided seven years of torment if he had listened to Daniel and repented in the first place. When the king finally repented, his kingdom was restored.

When King Nebuchadnezzar's son, Belshazzar, became king, he did not heed a warning given in a dream and refused to repent. He died just as Daniel's interpretation warned. If we are living in disobedience and willful sin, God often gives a warning to provide an opportunity for repentance. If we don't heed the warning, we will pay the consequences.

God also gives warnings in dreams for the purpose of intercession to save lives. Prayer can turn the tide on a disaster, as this story illustrates.

A woman had a dream that her niece was killed in a tragic car accident. Immediately she got out of bed and went to prayer interceding for her niece and praying God would spare her life. Later that night the woman received a phone call from her sister. Indeed her niece had been in a bad car accident but her life was spared. When God gives such a warning, someone must obey and stand in the gap in prayer. Satan's plan was to kill that young woman, but God's intercessor woke up in the night and prayed. God intervened and spared her life.

Now that we have explored the reasons why God speaks to us in dreams, I want to stress to you that not every dream is from God. The enemy can send tormenting dreams. Sometimes if we are over tired or stressed, the events or circumstances of the day may spill over into our dreams. And some believe that eating the wrong combination of foods before going to bed can even cause dreams. That is why it is so important to learn how to discern which dreams are from God and which ones aren't. In the next chapter I will share with you a seven-step process of how to receive a dream from God, and six keys to discern godly dreams.

Chapter 17

How To Receive A Dream From God

Daniel Jacobs, the young son of Mike and Cindy Jacobs, co-founders of Generals for Intercession Ministry, has a real heart for the Lord. For some reason the Lord gave Daniel a deep love for his Grandpa Johnson, Cindy's father who had died at forty-nine. He had not even been born when his grandfather died, but there was a spiritual bond. One day while at church camp when he was eleven years old, Daniel prayed, "Lord, I'd like to see my grandpa."

Daniel glanced over at a nearby fence and saw Jesus standing there with another man. (Remember the Scriptures in Acts and Joel that say, young men shall see visions?) Daniel didn't say anything. The man standing next to Jesus said, "Hello, Daniel. I'm your Granddad. I know the Daniel from the Bible. One day I'll introduce you to him."

Although Daniel had never seen his grandfather as a young man, he described him exactly to his mother who was crying big crocodile tears as Daniel excitedly shared with her on the phone what had happened. She asked Daniel what else her father had said to him.

He said, "Tell your mother I know all about her work for the Lord Jesus, and I'm really proud of her. Say hi to Mary for me." With those words the vision disappeared.

As Cindy related this story in her book, *The Voice of God*, she said, "How comforted I felt! What a wonderful feeling it is to know that Dad is looking over the grandstand of Heaven as part of that cloud of witnesses, cheering on his little girl. I don't know why God chose to answer my son that day. I'm sure other people have wanted to have just such an experience, but God didn't answer them in this way. I also know that we have to be aware of counterfeit spirits who want to deceive us — but I truly believe Daniel had a visitation that day and that it changed all of us."[1]

God still performs miracles today and He answers prayers when we pray. Now, I want you to know I am not advocating necromancy, calling people up from the dead. It is forbidden in the Scriptures. However, if the Lord chooses to answer a young boy's prayer through a vision, that's His business. At the transfiguration of Jesus on the mountain, Peter, James and John saw Elijah and Moses talking to Jesus and the disciples recognized who they were.

> **After six days Jesus took Peter, James and John with him and led them up a high mountain, where they were all alone. There he was transfigured before them. His clothes became dazzling white, whiter than anyone in the world could bleach them. And there appeared before them Elijah and Moses, who were talking with Jesus. Peter said to Jesus, "Rabbi, it is good for us to be here. Let us put up three shelters-one for you, one for Moses and one for Elijah." (He did not know what to say, they were so frightened.) Then a cloud appeared and enveloped them, and a voice came from the cloud: "This is my Son, whom I love. Listen to him!" Suddenly, when they looked around, they no longer saw anyone with them except Jesus.**
>
> **—Mark 9:2-8 (NIV)**

God still works through dreams and visions to answer our questions, to save those who are unsaved, to give us warnings and instructions, and to give us intercessory guidance on behalf of other people.

Perhaps you have never received a dream from the Lord, or perhaps you have and didn't recognize that it was from the Lord. Let me share with you how to·receive a dream from God with this seven-step process.

• *Step Number 1: Ask God to speak to you in a dream.*

If you want to receive a dream from the Lord, then simply *ask* Him. If you ask, He will answer as it says in this Scripture:

> "Ask and it will be given to you; seek and you will find; knock and the door will be opened to you. For everyone who asks receives; he who seeks finds; and to him who knocks, the door will be opened. Which of you, if his son asks for bread, will give him a stone? Or if he asks for a fish, will give him a snake? If you, then, though you are evil, know how to give good gifts to your children, how much more will your Father in heaven give good gifts to those who ask him."
>
> — Matthew 7:7-11 (NIV)

• *Step Number 2: Expect to receive.*

If you ask for a dream, do so with expectation that sooner or later God will give you that dream. Remember to be specific in what you ask, so God will be able to answer you.

• *Step Number 3: Be still when you first awaken.*

Sometimes we have dreams but we jump up out of bed so quickly we don't remember them. When you first wake up, wait to see if you remember anything. If you do, ask the Lord if it is from Him. If peace fills your heart, know that the dream is from Him. We need to be aware of Satan's counterfeits that come to torment us. If a dream fills you with fear and anxiety, it is not from the Lord.

• *Step Number 4: Write the details of the dream down and date it.*

Dreams are not necessarily to be taken literally. They have spiritual connotations and often the revelation unfolds to you over time. Dreams from the Lord are usually very vivid and in detail. If you don't write it down, you may not be able to remember the details later when the revelation comes.

• *Step Number 5: Pray for understanding and an interpretation of the dream.*

Every dream has a different interpretation. Some dreams are literal, some are spiritual and others may have both a literal and a spiritual meaning. Dreams are often symbolic. You don't want to be led astray in the interpretation. That is why you have to ask God to help you understand it. He will either reveal it to you or send someone to you who is gifted and qualified in interpreting dreams. It takes a great deal of discernment and spiritual maturity to interpret dreams so be careful to whom you listen.

We aren't able to go into depth about how to interpret a dream in this writing. It could be a book all by itself. There are some excellent anointed Christian books available on this subject. I have provided a list of suggested reading at the back of this book. Don't go out and buy any of those secular or occult books on dream interpretation, they will lead you into error and deception.

Be patient and wait upon the Lord. Sometimes it takes years for the meaning to be revealed such as in the case of Joseph in the Bible.

• *Step Number 6: Be careful with whom you share it.*

Remember, Joseph shared his dream with his brothers and they threw him in a pit. Later they sold him into slavery because they were so jealous of him. Other people may not understand the meaning of your dream and may talk you out of what God is trying to show you. Some may even be jealous and cause strife to rise up. Seek wisdom regarding a dream only from someone who is spiritually mature and trustworthy.

• *Step Number 7: Never rely on a dream as your sole source of guidance for a major decision.*

Be very cautious about using a dream to direct any major decisions in your life. A dream from God will never contradict the Scriptures, because God never contradicts His written Word. If it doesn't illustrate or illuminate the Scriptures for your specific situation, it is not from God.

The apostle James spoke about the difference between heavenly versus demonic wisdom in this Scripture:

> Who is wise and understanding among you? Let him show it by his good life, by deeds done in the humility that comes from wisdom. But if you harbor bitter envy and selfish ambition in your hearts, do not boast about it or deny the truth. Such "wisdom" does not come down from heaven but is earthly, unspiritual, of the devil. For where you have envy and selfish ambition, there you find disorder and every evil practice. But the wisdom that comes from heaven is first of all pure; then peace-loving, considerate, submissive, full of mercy and good fruit, impartial and sincere. Peacemakers who sow in peace raise a harvest of righteousness.
>
> —James 3:13-18 (NIV)

The key to using godly wisdom in making decisions is determining whether the action is taken in a peace-loving manner, in submission to God, and produces good fruit.

God warns us about false dreams and false prophets as this Scripture clearly states:

> If a prophet, or one who foretells by dreams, appears among you and announces to you a miraculous sign or wonder, and if the sign or wonder of which he has spoken takes place, and he says, "Let us follow other gods" — (gods you have not known) — "and let us worship them,"

> you must not listen to the words of that prophet
> or dreamer. The LORD your God is testing you
> to find out whether you love him with all your
> heart and with all your soul. It is the LORD your
> God you must follow, and him you must revere.
> Keep his commands and obey him; serve him
> and hold fast to him. That prophet or dreamer
> must be put to death, because he preached re-
> bellion against the LORD your God, who
> brought you out of Egypt and redeemed you from
> the land of slavery; he has tried to turn you from
> the way the LORD your God commanded you
> to follow. You must purge the evil from among
> you.
>
> —Deuteronomy 13:1-5 (NIV)

God is very serious about any false dream or prophet that leads people astray. Anything that adds to or detracts from the Word of God is suspect.

Joseph Smith claimed to have special revelation from God. He said an angel came to him and delivered golden tablets that were an update to the Gospel. An entire religious system was built upon a false dream given by a false prophet. Still today, many are being led into a Christ-less grave in eternity. If Joseph Smith had sought God's wisdom, Smith would have known that his revelation actually contradicted God's Holy Scriptures. He would never have penned another testament — the Book of Mormon — that teaches a *different* Jesus and a *different* gospel. Jesus was not a man that attained deity. Jesus was God, is God and always shall be God.

Jesus Christ is the *only* way to the Father, as He said in the Gospel of John:

> Jesus answered, "I am the way and the truth and the life. No one comes to the Father except through me."

> —John 14:6 (NIV)

There is no way to be born again by dying and being born on another planet. There is no way to be good enough to be god of your own planet. The only way to salvation and eternal life is through Jesus Christ. Joseph Smith's followers may be living good, moral lives, but they will never be good enough to attain perfection or eternal life without first acknowledging Jesus Christ as the Son of God. Jesus is the King of Kings and the Lord of Lords, and people must ask Him to live and dwell in their hearts. Any other way is deception that will take them to the pit of hell.

Some people may say, "Since there is such danger from false dreams, shouldn't we ignore all dreams?" No, we are only to ignore *false* dreams. Every once in a while we read about a good cop gone bad. He may have taken bribes, stolen some of the drugs he confiscated, or beaten a suspect. When it is revealed, the whole police force takes the flack. However, one bad cop doesn't mean all cops are bad. It's not the badge that made that one cop bad. It was one cop who used the badge falsely.

If the devil brings us false dreams and we begin to arrogantly speak them as if they are from God, we are like that cop gone bad. Dreams are not bad in themselves, and God can speak to us in dreams. Here are six questions to ask yourself to help you discern if a dream is from God or not:

1. Does it lead me to Jesus Christ and fill me with love for His people?

2. Does it promote righteousness and purity in my life?

3. Does it align itself with the clear and simple teachings of the Bible?

4. Does it strengthen my faith and fill me with a sense of destiny and honorable purpose in life?

5. Does it turn me from sin and selfishness to seek the Lord and serve Him in faithfulness and love?

6. Does it build up the body of Christ and equip believers to do the work of the ministry?[2]

If the answer to any of these questions is no, then the chances are the dream, vision or revelation is not from God.

God loves to speak to people who have these characteristics:

- Those who are available to hear and do His will.

- Those who are humble and submissive to Him.

- Those who know His voice and are prompt to obey and act on His words.

Are You Available?

You may not feel like you have much ability, but if you have availability, God will speak to you. The problem is, it is so tough nowadays to be available to God because we're so busy working for God. A modern day prophet, Paul Cain, said, "What if you baked God apple pies all of your life? What if you served Him every day by baking apple pies and when you came to the end of your life, you discovered God doesn't even like apple pie? You would have wasted your entire life doing something God did not even want you to do."[3]

The key is availability. Jesus was always available to His Father. He said:

> "I have many things to say and to judge concerning you, but He who sent Me is true; and I speak to the world those things which I heard from Him." They did not understand that He spoke to them of the Father. Then Jesus said to them, "When you lift up the Son of Man, then

> you will know that I am He, and that I do noth-
> ing of Myself; but as My Father taught Me, I
> speak these things. And He who sent Me is with
> Me. The Father has not left Me alone, for I al-
> ways do those things that please Him."
>
> —John 8:26-29

Jesus was never in a rush. He didn't have to carry His Daytimer™ to keep Him on schedule. He didn't have to sit up all night writing His sermon for the next day. He was just available to do His Father's will, and the Holy Spirit gave Him the words to speak.

I used to worry myself sick about my Sunday morning sermon and couldn't sleep on Saturday night. My stomach would be in knots because I wanted everything to be perfect. Now, if my message doesn't come from Heaven by Saturday night, I don't even worry about it. I say, "Lord, It'll come in the morning. I'm going to bed."

God just wants us to be available to Him. He speaks to those who say to Him first thing in the morning, "Lord, I just want to make myself available to please You today. I ask You to speak to me, to let me know what's on Your heart so I can be part of what You're doing. I don't want to bake you an apple pie if you don't like apple pie."

Are You Humble?

God speaks to the humble but deals with the proud from afar. The apostle Paul had many revelations, dreams and visions, including a trip to Heaven and back, but he said:

> For I am the least of the apostles and do not even deserve to be called an apostle...
>
> — 1 Corinthians 15:9 (NIV)

God loves to reveal things to people who stay in a spirit of humility. The greatest men of God in the Bible were the humblest of God's servants. Moses was said to be the most humble man on earth, and God severely rebuked his sister, Miriam, for speaking against His servant, Moses. Let's read what God said:

> Miriam and Aaron began to talk against Moses because of his Cushite wife, for he had married a Cushite. "Has the LORD spoken only through Moses?" they asked. "Hasn't he also spoken through us?" And the LORD heard this. (Now Moses was a very humble man, more humble than anyone else on the face of the earth.) At once the LORD said to Moses, Aaron and Miriam, "Come out to the Tent of Meeting, all three of you." So the three of them came out. Then the LORD came down in a pillar of cloud; he stood at the entrance to the Tent and summoned Aaron and Miriam. When both of them stepped forward, he said, "Listen to my words: 'When a prophet of the LORD is among you, I reveal myself to him in visions; I speak to him in dreams. But this is not true of my servant

> Moses; he is faithful in all my house. With him I
> speak face to face, clearly and not in riddles; he
> sees the form of the LORD. Why then were you
> not afraid to speak against my servant Moses'"
>
> —Numbers 12:1-8 (NIV)

There was such an intimacy between Moses and
God that God spoke to Moses like a friend, face to
face. When Moses came down off the mountain after
talking with God, he had to wear a veil over his face
because his face shone with God's glory.

God has no patience with the spiritually proud
and arrogant. He spoke quite clearly how He felt
about this in Psalm 138:

> Though the LORD is on high, he looks upon the
> lowly, but the proud he knows from afar.
>
> —Psalm 138:6 (NIV)

A few years ago I was walking out the back of the
church at the close of the service, and a lady greeted
me.

"Hello, Pastor Williams. My name is Kay (not her
real name)."

"Nice to meet you. I'm glad you were here today."

"I want you to know, I'm a prophetess."

All of a sudden buzzers started going off in my
spirit. I've had dealings with self-proclaimed proph-

ets and prophetesses before, but it's like the good cop, bad cop story. One false prophet doesn't mean all prophets are in error, so I listened patiently.

"I want to tell you that before the end of December, there is going to be a terrible earthquake down the middle of Michigan. Also, you can't let your mission team go to Venezuela. Ten of them are going to be shot by terrorists. God showed me this."

I prayed about it and felt very comfortable sending our mission team off to Venezuela. They had a wonderful, fruitful trip with no mishaps. December came and went with no earthquake. It wasn't hard to discern that Kay was a false prophet, speaking in the name of the Lord things that did not come to pass. She wrote me two letters and rebuked me for not following her directions. Her manner was total arrogance because I did not accept her as a prophetess. God does not speak to those who are arrogant.

On another occasion, a prophet came up to me and said, "Pastor, I've just been having some thoughts I believe are from the Lord. Now see if this confirms anything with you." He shared in a very humble way what he heard the Lord saying.

Some time later, two of our church leaders and I went out of town to seek direction for the church. While we were praying in the hotel, we had a vision of our church as a ship stuck on a sandbar. We were expending a lot of energy, but the ship wasn't going anywhere. We started throwing over excess baggage until the ship floated off the sandbar. We poured power to the engines and away we went. We had guidance from this vision that we needed to cut away what we call "Ishmael" ministries, that are born of the flesh rather than of the Spirit.

When we returned, this same prophet came up to me and said, "Pastor, see if this bears witness to you. Last night while I was praying, the Lord showed me our church as a ship caught on a sandbar . . .." " He went on and prophesied the whole vision we had seen in the hotel as we prayed. This confirmed to my heart that this man was hearing from God, bringing confirmation to his pastor. He did it with such a spirit of humility I knew it was God.

When a person sees something wrong with everyone else, and the church, and calls it discernment; it is arrogance, not discernment. God loves His church and He doesn't send prophets to condemn, find fault and tear down. A true prophet humbly builds up and edifies the church. That isn't to say the Lord may not send a word of correction or instruction through a prophet, but it is always given in a spirit of love and humility for the purpose of building up, not tearing down.

God doesn't speak to the proud and haughty because He can't trust them, and neither can you or I. If you truly want to hear from the Lord, you must humble yourself before Him.

Do You Hear And Obey?

God doesn't speak to people who ignore what He says. He speaks to people who hear and obey His voice *and* His written Word. He knows that if you don't obey His written Word, you'll never obey His spoken words. A good example is someone who prays and asks the Lord to give him revelation about financial investments, but doesn't hear anything from God. The first question I would ask is whether that person is tithing and giving offerings unto the Lord. If not, he can't expect the Lord to answer his prayer. God will not speak any further beyond your obedience to His written Word — the Bible.

God loves to speak to those with whom He shares an intimate relationship, because they recognize His voice and obey without question.

I love my wife and I know her voice. However, before I knew Mary Jo very well, one of her sisters could have called and I wouldn't have been able to tell which one it was. After I met Mary Jo and she was going to Bible School in Dallas, we spent hours and hours on the phone talking long distance about anything and everything. Before long I knew her voice, and her sisters couldn't fool me on the phone anymore.

Mary Jo could come to church in a disguise and fool me, until I heard her speak. Once we are used to talking with God about anything and everything in life, He can show up packaged in a way in which we are not accustomed, but we will still know His voice when He speaks. God wants us to be so intimate with Him that we know His voice regardless of how He is packaged, even if He comes incognito.

What Are Your Motives?

If you want to hear the voice of the Lord, be sure to check your motives. Your motives should be to be more intimate with Him and to know Him better so you can please Him.

As a pastor, I always pray for three specific spiritual gifts: words of wisdom, discerning of spirits and the gift of faith. Sometimes I check my motives and ask myself, "Why do I want to flow in the supernatural. Why do I want to know something about somebody that isn't in my notes? Why do I want people to feel like I'm reading their mail?" If it is because I want people to think I'm an awesome minister or to say, "Isn't he wonderful?" or "Oh, he's great, isn't he?" I have to say, "God, get that haughty attitude out of me!"

It has been a long time since I felt that way. Now I pray, "Lord, I want words of wisdom, words of knowledge and prophetic words so I can know what is on Your heart and become more intimate with you. I want to please You today. What is it You want me to be available for today?" I no longer worry whether my sermons will be good or not, because my only desire is to please the Lord. If I'm pleasing Him, then I know the greatest numbers of people are being touched and helped.

Dreams are subjective but God's Word is objective. God's Word is truth. Heaven and earth will pass away, but God's Word will never pass away. Availability, humility and obedience, bring divine revelation to our lives as we get to know the voice of God. A person who says, "God, I'm available to You, any way You need me today, and I'm ready to obey your voice," develops a hearing heart.

"What you hear with your natural ears isn't as important as what you hear God speaking to your heart. As you speak what you hear in your heart, you encourage and build up yourself and other believers."

Chapter 18

The Importance Of A Hearing Heart

Can you imagine being blind and slalom skiing down a steep slope? An amazing special presentation was aired prior to the last winter Olympics featuring blind skiers doing just that. Each blind skier was paired with a sighted skier who gave very specific voice commands to his or her blind partner – left, right, left, right. The blind skier did exactly what the sighted partner said to do and skied smoothly down the slope weaving in and out of the slalom gates. This unbelievable feat required complete trust in the sighted skier's commands and absolute, unquestioning obedience on the part of the blind skier.

Skiing Blind

Isn't that the way we go through life? We can't see what is up ahead and must rely on Someone (the

Holy Spirit) Who sees the beginning from the end to say, "Left, right, left." He sees danger straight ahead and guides us around the icy spots or drop offs that would cause us to fall or veer off course and slam into a tree.

Skiing is dangerous sport even for a sighted skier, as evidenced by the deaths of another Kennedy son and Senator Sonny Bono. Both of these men were excellent skiers, and yet they were killed when each one veered off the slope and hit a tree. Now imagine what it would be like to be skiing blindly down a slope at fifty or sixty miles an hour trusting that the commands someone is calling out will keep you out of danger? The faster we go through life, the more dangerous it is *not* to hear the voice of the Lord.

Love Is The Guidance System

Throughout this book we have talked about the Holy Spirit's guidance system. As we continue our study on hearing, knowing, and understanding the voice of the Lord, let's read one of the best-known chapters in the Bible, often called "the love chapter."

> Though I speak with the tongues of men and of angels, but have not love, I have become sounding brass or a clanging cymbal. And though I have *the gift of* prophecy, and understand all mysteries and all knowledge, and though I have all faith, so that I could remove mountains, but have not love, I am nothing. And though I be-

stow all my goods to feed *the poor*, and though I give my body to be burned, but have not love, it profits me nothing. Love suffers long *and* is kind; love does not envy; love does not parade itself, is not puffed up; does not behave rudely, does not seek its own, is not provoked, thinks no evil; does not rejoice in iniquity, but rejoices in the truth; bears all things, believes all things, hopes all things, endures all things.

—1 Corinthians 13:1-7

This passage is telling us that the motivation for using our spiritual gifts is always love. In the King James Version we see the word, "charity," used for love, which is the Greek word "agape," meaning "affection or benevolence; specifically a love-feast." This is the deepest form of love possible.[1]

Feed The Sheep, Don't Pick Their Lice

I remember visiting a church one time and looking at the people, I felt tremendous love for them. I didn't even know these people but my heart was filled with love for them. As the pastor was preaching I was shocked at the way he was beating them up with his words. I sat there thinking, *"My goodness, these people go to their jobs and get ridiculed, criticized, talked about and persecuted. Then they come to church and the preacher beats them up from the pulpit!"*

I said, "Lord, forgive me for being critical of that pastor."

The Lord said, "No, you're not being critical of the pastor. I'm showing you something."

"What are You showing me, Lord?"

"I'm showing you that your motivation to be a minister is because you really do love the flock. You really love My people. That is why I showed you My love for these people through you even though you don't know them. You know they are My sheep, and they are being beaten up by someone who calls himself a shepherd."

The Lord instructed me never to beat up the sheep. That's when I got the phrase, "Feed the sheep, don't pick their lice." Love is the motivator for feeding the sheep.

Love Never Fails

The following verses refer to prophecy, tongues and knowledge. In the Greek language the phrase, "that which is perfect is come," is in the masculine speaking of a person. In other words, when a certain person, which is perfect, has come, we won't need prophecy or any special gifts because we will be with that person — Jesus Christ. In looking at this chapter in context with the following two chapters, we see in chapter 15 the apostle Paul is speaking of the second coming of Christ.

> Love never fails. But whether *there are* prophe-
> cies, they will fail; whether *there are* tongues,
> they will cease; whether *there is* knowledge, it
> will vanish away. For we know in part and we
> prophesy in part. But when that which is per-
> fect has come, then that which is in part will be
> done away.
>
> —1 Corinthians 13:8-10

Reading the remainder of the chapter we see that before Jesus comes again for us, we are like children in need of guidance and special gifts. We can't see clearly now, but when we see Him face-to-face, each of us will become a mature man or woman. In the meantime we are to abide in and be motivated by His love:

> When I was a child, I spoke as a child, I under-
> stood as a child, I thought as a child; but when I
> became a man, I put away childish things. For
> now we see in a mirror, dimly, but then face to
> face. Now I know in part, but then I shall know
> just as I also am known. And now abide faith,
> hope, love, these three; but the greatest of these
> *is* love.
>
> —1 Corinthians 13:11-13

Paul is saying to let love be your motivation in desiring spiritual gifts, especially prophecy, as he explains here in the beginning of chapter fourteen:

> Pursue love, and desire spiritual *gifts*, but espe-
> cially that you may prophesy.
>
> —1 Corinthians 14:1

Before we go any further, let me explain the word, "prophesy," in this verse. In this context prophesy refers to God speaking to a person's heart, and that person speaking out what God speaks to his or her heart. This is known as New Testament or, "simple" prophecy.

For example, in your private devotions you are praying when God begins to speak certain thoughts into your heart. As you speak these thoughts out loud, it becomes a prophetic word. That is what we call, "simple prophecy." Every believer can benefit by prophesying.

Who Is A Prophet?

Simple prophecy is not to be confused with the office of a prophet spoken of in Ephesians 4:11-13:

> It was he who gave some to be apostles, some to be prophets, some to be evangelists, and some to be pastors and teachers, to prepare God's people for works of service, so that the body of Christ may be built up until we all reach unity in the faith and in the knowledge of the Son of God and become mature, attaining to the whole measure of the fullness of Christ.
>
> —Ephesians 4:11-13 (NIV)

Just because you can hear God's voice and speak it out, does not mean you are called to the office of a prophet. Old Testament prophets that operated in the office of a prophet were such men as Samuel, Isaiah,

Daniel, Ezekiel and Jeremiah. Some modern day prophets are Paul Cain, Dick Mills, Chuck Pierce and Cindy Jacobs, just to name a few. The spiritual gifts are for everyone, but Jesus specifically calls a person to the office of apostle, prophet, evangelist, pastor or teacher. The spiritual gifts and offices spoken of in this passage, though different, are still in operation today, and will continue to be until we all come into the unity of faith. It hasn't happened yet, but when it does, Jesus will return and we will be with the One Who is Perfect.

Why We Need A Hearing Heart

In the following passage, Paul is emphasizing the importance of prophecy — of having a hearing heart:

> For he who speaks in a tongue does not speak to men but to God, for no one understands *him*; however, in the spirit he speaks mysteries. But he who prophesies speaks edification and exhortation and comfort to men. He who speaks in a tongue edifies himself, but he who prophesies edifies the church. I wish you all spoke with tongues, but even more that you prophesied; for he who prophesies *is* greater than he who speaks with tongues, unless indeed he interprets, that the church may receive edification.
>
> —1 Corinthians 14:2-5

What you hear with your natural ears isn't as important as what you hear God speaking to your heart or spirit. Then as you speak what you hear in your heart, you encourage and build up yourself and other believers.

When God Speaks, Who Listens?

The problem is not trying to get God to speak to us. He is always speaking to us. The key is to develop ears to hear what the Lord is saying to your heart. Many of us were raised in churches that did not embrace the concept that God still speaks to people or that spiritual gifts are for today. We were told God said all He was going to say before 96 A.D. because once His Book was written, He had no more reason to speak. The Bible is the plumb line by which we judge every word that may come to us, but He still speaks to us.

Some people hear God speak to them all the time, and others go through life saying, "Oh, I don't hear God saying anything." It was no different when Jesus walked on the earth. At His baptism God spoke and said, "This is My beloved Son, in whom I am well pleased," (Matthew 3:17). At His transfiguration God spoke and said, "This is My beloved Son. Hear Him!" (Mark 9:7). Some people who were there heard the words so clearly they were able to record them for us to read today. Others nearby probably didn't hear anything except a clap of thunder. God speaks to those who have ears to hear.

A Life Transformed

I have talked a lot about Cindy Jacobs because she is an amazing person. I highly recommend her book, *The Voice of God*, if you want to learn more about hearing and understanding the voice of God, especially as it relates to prophecy. Here is a story that illustrates how a life can be transformed by having a hearing heart.

Cindy was taking her rental car back to the Los Angeles airport. As she pulled into a gas station to fill it up with gas, she noticed an African-American man standing there shabbily dressed with a pail of water and a squeegee in his hand. He said, "Lady, can I wash your windows for you?"

"No, thanks, it's a rental car. I'm taking it back, and they will wash it anyway so there's no sense in doing that." She went on into the station to pay for her gas.

When she came back out the man was still standing there, and the Lord spoke something to Cindy's heart. She looked at the man and said, "You know, even though I don't need the windows washed, there is something I need to tell you. There's a mighty call of God on your life. You've been in a place of imprisonment, and your parents and grandparents are praying for you and you need to go home. You need to go home to God."

The man dropped his pail, his eyes opened up like pumpkin pies and he started crying. He said, "Tha-that's true. Everything you said! I just got out of prison, and when I was a little boy I used to kneel at the altar and weep, and my grandfather would pray for me and say, 'One day you're going to preach the Gospel and be a mighty man of God.'"

The young man's eyes brightened and he said, "Lady, I'm going home. I'm going to call my parents and tell them I'm coming home. I'm going home to the Lord and to my parents today." I'm giving up this life and going home today. I'm going to fulfill my destiny!"[2]

Communication Is A Privilege

Do you see how a word from the Lord can absolutely penetrate the soul of another human being and change that person's life forever? The greatest privilege we have on earth is communing and communicating with the Creator. It is two-way communication — we talk to Him and He talks to us. He says, "Turn right, left, right." He reminds us that we're looking at this life through a glass darkly, but He sees the beginning from the end.

God's voice is a creative voice. The earth was void and without form, but when He spoke and said, "Let there be light," there was a sun, a moon and billions of stars to light the sky. He said, "Let the earth bring forth grass," and seeds sprouted into green vegetation and trees grew to yield fruit. He said, "Let Us make man in Our image," and He created man and woman. The worlds were formed as God spoke. He took nothing and turned it into something simply by speaking it forth.

God's voice is still creative as He *speaks* into our lives. His words have energy, bringing life to hopes and dreams and difficult or impossible situations. Jesus is the Living Word, and He doesn't just speak through the written Word of the Scriptures. When Jesus returned to Heaven, He left the Holy Spirit here to comfort us and guide us into all truth. God speaks to us through His Spirit.

Silence Destroys Intimacy

Wouldn't it be awful to be married to someone that never talked to you? Lack of communication in one form or another is the number one cause of divorce, and the primary cause of teenagers getting into trouble with drugs and alcohol.

What if you had a spouse that never said a word to you, just every once in a while left you a note?

What about a parent that never spoke to a child and just left notes saying, "Wipe your feet. Take off your shoes. Clean your room. Feed the dog?" Believe it or not, in today's fast paced society this actually happens in some families. Schedules are so hectic that everyone "passes in the night," barely seeing or speaking to each other for days at a time. They just leave notes on the refrigerator door. It is a disaster waiting to happen. Intimacy between spouses and between parents and children has almost become a thing of the past. As a result the family unit is disintegrating right before our eyes.

Now think about this. What if we had a God that never spoke to His children? Some people believe this is true, and we have seen the results of dead religion in the church for too many years. We need to hear the creative voice of God to keep love alive in our hearts. We need to have the spiritual gifts operating in our lives to be able to hear His voice. We need to have ears to hear *and* a hearing heart to be directed and guided away from danger, and into our destiny.

God's Creative Voice

Did you know that every miracle recorded in the Bible was prefaced by the creative voice of God speaking it? He spoke it *before* it happened. The first miracle Jesus performed, as recorded by the apostle, John, was at a wedding feast in Cana. It was probably the wedding of a close family friend because Jesus' mother was there, and Jesus and all the disciples were invited.

When the host ran out of wine at the reception, Jesus' mother said to her son, "They have no wine." She had an expectation that He could take care of the problem. He tried to get out of it but, like most mothers, she wasn't to be put off. She pointed to her son and said to the servants, "Whatever He says to you, do it." That is good advice, isn't it? If He speaks, you do it!

Let's read what Jesus told the servants to do in this Scripture:

> Jesus said to the servants, "Fill the jars with water"; so they filled them to the brim. Then he told them, "Now draw some out and take it to the master of the banquet." They did so, and the master of the banquet tasted the water that had been turned into wine. He did not realize where it had come from, though the servants who had drawn the water knew. Then he called the bridegroom aside and said, "Everyone brings out the choice wine first and then the cheaper wine after the guests have had too much to drink; but you have saved the best till now."
>
> —John 2:7-10 (NIV)

When the wine was poured into the glasses of the guests, it was the best wine they had ever tasted in their lives. Jesus took that which was ordinary and spoke a word. His creative voice turned ordinary water into fine, new wine. This proves Jesus can take someone common like me, and by speaking a word into my life, He can make me into someone extraordinary. He can do the same with you.

Speaking As Jesus Spoke

Think about the creative voice of Jesus. Miracles didn't just happen. It took the creative voice of God spoken with authority to produce each miracle. Go back and study the miracles of the Bible like I did, and you will find it is true. The disciples followed after Jesus and learned how to speak in the same manner as we read here:

> Then Peter said, Silver and gold have I none; but such as I have give I thee: In the name of Jesus Christ of Nazareth rise up and walk. And he took him by the right hand, and lifted him up: and immediately his feet and ankle bones received strength. And he leaping up stood, and walked, and entered with them into the temple, walking, and leaping, and praising God. And all the people saw him walking and praising God.
>
> —Acts 3:6-9 (KJV)

A prophetic, creative word spoken by Peter, brought a man who had been crippled for forty years to his feet, leaping and praising God. Isn't that awesome? It still happens today. I've seen it happen in Africa.

Why Does It Happen In Africa?

Have you ever wondered why such creative miracles are common in Africa but not in the Western world? One reason is that the intellectual mindset of Western thinking has eroded the power of simple faith. Another reason is that church doctrine has taught us it can't happen today, so it doesn't. In Africa when I say something by the Spirit of God, the people believe and obey, and miracles happen. In other words, they have hearing hearts.

I was holding a citywide crusade in Mitchell's Plain, Africa. The auditorium was packed that night and I was preaching on the subject of miracles. I had prayed that afternoon that God would speak to me prophetically, so that I would hear God's voice and know exactly the right words to say.

While I was preaching I began seeing things in the Spirit. It was like watching a movie on a transparent screen. I saw a man, not with my natural eyes, with a twisted leg from an old injury. It was bent at an angle and he couldn't straighten it out, so he walked in a pretty painful manner. I saw another lady in the Spirit, in pain with what looked like fists pounding on her heart. I realized this must be the voice of God giving me words of knowledge. I said, "The Lord is showing me there is a man here whose leg is twisted at an angle from an injury. You haven't been able to straighten it out or have normal movement in it since the injury. If you'll stand up and kick that leg out straight right now, it will be freed up."

A man hopped up and kicked his leg out straight. Suddenly he was leaping and running, and people started screaming in the auditorium. People who knew the man said he had not been able to do that since his injury.

At the same time, a little lady about sixty years old was smiling and crying. She said she had been experiencing pain in her chest for several months and now it was all gone. God healed her heart. A prophetic word of knowledge spoken by God's anointed servant, mixed with the faith of a crippled man and a hurting woman, resulted in miraculous healings. People in Africa come to those meetings expecting miracles, and God shows up.

Water Speaks Life

Here is another example of how God speaks a creative word today. Keith and Tim worked with YWAM, Youth with a Mission. They had a heart for reaching people in the 10/40 window of the Middle East, but there are some nations Christians are barred from entering. They wondered how they could get into these nations, and God gave them a plan.

They joined the United Nations' Wells of Life Program to go in and dig water wells for the Kurdish people in northern Iraq. Saddam Hussein had wiped out the Kurdish villages and destroyed their water wells by pouring concrete down some and blowing others up with bombs. In many villages all they had was a pond of thick, gray muddy water. Over two million Kurdish people were displaced and many were dying. The situation was desperate.

The well-drilling team searched for water, drilling in several locations, but was unable to hit water. Everyone was discouraged and frustrated. The Kurds are Muslim people, but Keith and Tim kept praying, "God, show us how we can demonstrate to them that Jesus is the way, the truth and the life, that He is the Savior. Help us show them Your love."

Keith and Tim felt led to climb up a nearby hilltop to pray. The Kurdish chief followed them with an interpreter. Upon reaching the hilltop, Keith and Tim bowed their heads and prayed, "Father, in the name of Jesus, these people desperately need water. Please show us where to drill for water that they might see that You care for them."

Keith looked up and said, "Tim, I think the Lord is telling us to drill right here on this hilltop."

Tim said, "I just got that same impression."

When they shared this plan with the chief through the interpreter, the chief went berserk. He said, "Oh, everyone knows the water base is much lower. It is stupid to drill on a hilltop. It is only going to provide more disappointment and discouragement for my people."

They discussed it back and forth rather heatedly as Keith and Tim assured the chief that the God of Heaven through His Son, Jesus Christ, cares about the Kurdish people, and said to drill right there on the hilltop. Finally the chief agreed.

Keith and Tim got the drilling equipment set up. They drilled only four feet and hit some sort of artesian well. Water was spewing high into the air. The pressure in the well was so great they were able to build a system that supplied water to the entire village. The light of the Gospel of Jesus Christ came to northern Iraq because of a creative prophetic word from God.[3]

When we develop a hearing heart, *and* then *do* what the Spirit tells us to do, we will see the miraculous power of God released. The servants at the wedding feast in Cana did exactly what Jesus told them to do, and water was miraculously turned into fine wine. Keith and Tim did what the Lord told them to do, and against all logical reason drilled a well on top of a hill. Sometimes what God tells us to do doesn't fit with our plan, but I have learned God's plan is always better.

No One-way Conversations

Developing ears to hear and a hearing heart are not as difficult as you might think. You were created to communicate with God. It is His desire to listen to you *and* to talk with you. He doesn't believe in one-way telephone calls. God has a definite, unique and specific plan for each of our lives. If He doesn't speak, how can we discover that plan? When He speaks, He expects us to listen and do what He tells us to do. One of the greatest compliments we can pay to God as an act of worship, is to listen to what He has to say in His written Word *and* by His Spirit. Listening means we must be still and let Him do the talking.

Jesus tells us over and over again in His Word how important it is to have a hearing heart. As you listen with your heart, you will hear His creative voice guiding and protecting you in your daily walk. You will be motivated by His love to utilize your spiritual gifts and speak out what He is saying, to lift up and help others in the body of Christ. You will also discover what His plan is for your own life, and learn how to fulfill your destiny.

God is speaking today. His voice is creative and redemptive. Prophecy is not something to fear. It is something to embrace. It brings hope to discouraged lives and builds something beautiful out of ruins. If He can speak and turn water into wine, he can speak to you prophetically and turn you into something extraordinary, with a call and a destiny to change this world for Jesus.

Chapter 19

Why All The Fuss About Prophecy?

Chuck Pierce was preparing to go to a conference in California when he looked over at one of his staff members at the World Prayer Center. She happened to be the daughter of Dr. C. Peter Wagner. Chuck said to her, "Rebecca, you need to be at the conference because your husband is going to be there."

Rebecca looked at him rather surprised and said, "Well, okay but I'm not registered, and I don't have any reservations."

Rebecca was not married and had gone through a painful period in her life. She was not planning to go to the conference but, when Chuck Pierce spoke to her, she knew He was hearing the voice of God. She made flight reservations while Chuck called the hotel to book her a room, only to be told there were no rooms available. Chuck was not going to be put off. He said, "Lady, the person for whom I am making this reservation is the daughter of the conference leader, and besides that she is supposed to meet her husband there."

The reservation clerk did not realize the significance of what Chuck had just spoken, but said, "Let me check again." She came back on the line and said, "Someone just cancelled a reservation and I can book that room as you requested."

Rebecca attended that conference and met Jack, the man God had prepared to be her husband. She and Jack were married and have been serving the Lord together ever since, because a trusted servant of God heard His creative voice and spoke forth the prophecy. Rebecca knew the importance of prophecy — it is the voice of God, and it releases life and power into specific circumstances. She acted in faith on the word of prophecy spoken by Chuck and was rewarded for her obedience.

The Purposes Of Prophecy

We all need to recognize the value and purposes of simple prophecy, which are edification, exhortation, comfort, and strategies for warfare and direction. Let's examine each of these benefits.

• *Benefit Number 1: Edification*

Edification builds character in the church and in individual lives that may be in ruin. Sometimes it is necessary to tear down something that is being built on the wrong foundation, but the Holy Spirit always provides what is needed to build it back up on the right foundation. Love is the key to building up versus tearing down. The prophetic word Cindy Jacobs gave to the man at the gas station who had been in prison is a good example of an edifying word.

• *Benefit Number 2: Exhortation*

Exhortation is a motivating force or warning that brings direction and hope. It encourages or motivates people to do great things for God. Remember, it never leaves you without hope. James Robison's mother received such a word from the Lord when she was so desperate she didn't know which way to turn. It gave her hope to proceed with the pregnancy, and James has fulfilled the word the Lord spoke to her while he was still in her womb. He has brought great joy to many people.

• *Benefit Number 3: Comfort*

God longs to comfort His hurting children. His comfort brings strength, breaking the chains of discouragement, hopelessness and anguish. Jesus called the Holy Spirit, the "Comforter." He is the One Who empowers, strengthens and brings peace to your heart. God knows you face struggles, and He wants to bring comfort to your heart and let you know He's not done with you. He is still working with you. The good work He has begun, He will finish even though you may have taken a detour.

• *Benefit Number 4: Strategies of Warfare*

Paul wrote to young Timothy about the value of prophecies to provide strategies for warfare as we read here:

> This charge I commit unto thee, son Timothy, according to the prophecies which went before on thee, that thou by them mightest war a good warfare.
>
> —1 Timothy 1:18 (KJV)

God spoke and gave Joshua the strategy for taking Jericho. It is an exciting story. Let's read what God said to Joshua:

> Then the LORD said to Joshua, "See, I have delivered Jericho into your hands, along with its king and its fighting men. March around the city once with all the armed men. Do this for six days. Have seven priests carry trumpets of rams' horns in front of the ark. On the seventh day, march around the city seven times, with the priests blowing the trumpets. When you hear them sound a long blast on the trumpets, have all the people give a loud shout; then the wall of the

city will collapse and the people will go up, every man straight in."

—Joshua 6:2-5 (NIV)

Joshua and his army obeyed God's instructions to the letter, and on the seventh day when they blew the trumpets and shouted in one accord, the walls of Jericho collapsed. To put the size of these walls in perspective, they were so thick a warrior could ride around the top of the wall with a horse and chariot and pass another chariot coming from the other direction. With one mighty shout those monstrous walls were obliterated.

I visited the Holy Land recently and we went to the excavated site where the wall of Jericho once stood. The only piece of the wall left was the stone of Rahab's house. She was the woman who hid the two spies and helped the people of Israel. She was told to tie a red cord on her window to identify her house. Everything else was destroyed.

Strategies For Today

God is giving strategies to His people today as well. Apostolic leader and prophet, Chuck Pierce, director of the World Prayer Center in Colorado Springs, recently directed a prayer journey focusing on major financial centers throughout the world. The Lord has given prayer intercessors specific strategies for taking back the ground stolen by the enemy and bringing restoration to peoples and nations.

Three of the cities they "prayer-walked" were Berlin, Warsaw, and Zurich in that order. This was a strategic pattern as they went from the place of Nazi government, to the place where most of the treasure and talent was plundered from the Jews, to the place where much of this treasure is now stored. While they were in Berlin praying, Germany's president, an evangelical Christian, was in Israel delivering an historic address to the Israeli parliament, touring the Holocaust Memorial and asking forgiveness for the Holocaust. After the prayer team's return to the US, nine billion dollars was released to be returned to Jewish people who were robbed of wealth in World War II. As well, Swiss banks and German industries have agreed to make restitution to the Jews who were robbed or worked as slaves during Hitler's reign of terror. God's strategies provide breakthroughs in miraculous ways.[1]

• *Benefit Number 5: Direction*

Prophecy often provides direction to our lives. I was 27 years old and unmarried. In my family, that meant every time I went to a family reunion people always said, "Are you married yet?" They just had to say it even though they knew I wasn't. (That's when you just want to slap them. So what if they are old and wrinkled!)

I remember praying, "God, I don't care. I will be celibate all my life if that is what You want. My only desire is to please You." I laid that before the Lord. Just then out of my spirit came these words, "You'll be married by next summer."

Man of faith that I was, the next words out of my mouth were, "I rebuke you, devil. I just laid this out before the Lord. I gave this desire to the Lord."

In His love and patience, God again said, "You'll be married by next summer.

"Lord, is that you?"

"You'll be married by next summer."

"This is August. How am I going to be married by next summer? I don't even have anybody in the picture."

Do you ever argue with God when He is trying to tell you something that is really what you want in the first place? It is a favorite tactic of the enemy to try to come and steal the Word from us. Sometimes we need to pray, "Lord, help my unbelief!"

Meanwhile, Mary Jo was with Youth With a Mission at one of those "real hard" mission fields, Hawaii. Her holy desire was to serve the Lord, and He was her first love. She wasn't looking for a husband. Late one evening, in the middle of the night, Mary Jo's roommate sat straight up in bed and said, "Thus saith the Lord, 'Mary Jo, I say unto thee that I have prepared a man for you, and thou shall marry him by next summer.'"

Mary Jo was listening to this prophecy coming from the girl in the bed across the room and thinking, What in the world is going on? The next morning she said to her roommate, "Now would you explain to me what you were talking about last night?"

"What do you mean what was I talking about?"

"You told me I was going to be married by next summer."

"Well, I don't remember that." She had prophesied in her sleep.

In August, Mary Jo came home to Michigan. She and a friend decided to stop over and visit their old Bible study teacher. My doorbell rang and when I opened it, there stood Mary Jo.

"Is that you?"

Mary Jo looked me right in the eye and said, "Is that you?"

"Yeah, welcome home."

I was conducting a baptismal service in the Grand River that day. I asked Mary Jo if she wanted to go along.

"Sure," she said, "but I don't have anything to wear."

Now you wanted to dress appropriately for the Grand River. That was when you didn't know what was going to go floating by in the river while you were baptizing people. I pulled out a pair of shorts and a sweatshirt for her to borrow that were way too big. She got a ride down to the river and watched us baptizing.

You know in the book of Acts how people were baptized and came up speaking in tongues and prophesying. Well, I baptized Rick Ledesma that day, and when he came up out of the water, he said, "I think God is calling you and Mary Jo to be a team."

Sixteen days before the following summer, Mary Jo and I were married as it had been prophesied. I had prophesized it to myself from the word the Lord spoke to me. Mary Jo's roommate had prophesied to her in the middle of the night. Then Rick came up out of the water prophesying it in a casual word. God gave us direction through prophecy.

Stay Away From Fruits, Flakes And Nuts

You may not have embraced the concept of God speaking to individuals today, but I hope reading this book has answered many of the questions you have had about it. I am the first to admit there are plenty of fruit, nuts and flakes out there, giving prophecy a bad name; just like the lady who told me an earthquake was going to hit Michigan and our mission team was going to be killed by terrorists. However, just because there are some immature and misguided people trying to speak in the name of the Lord, we shouldn't turn our backs on the value of prophecy. As always we should examine what the Bible says about such things as it says here:

> Do not smother the Holy Spirit. Do not scoff at those who prophesy, but test everything that is said to be sure it is true, and if it is, then accept it. Keep away from every kind of evil. May the God of peace himself make you entirely pure and devoted to God; and may your spirit and soul and body be kept strong and blameless until that day when our Lord Jesus Christ comes back again.
>
> —1 Thessalonians 5:19-23 (TLB)

The fact there is a counterfeit proves there is a genuine, and I want the genuine. One of the reasons I felt compelled to write this book is because it is my desire that all of God's people would prophesy —

hear the voice of the Lord, and have the ability to articulate His voice. We shouldn't fear prophecy.

God Loves Diversity

One reason people are afraid to speak a word from the Lord is because they are afraid they won't say it right. We all talk differently. My voice has a specific pattern that nobody else's voice in the world has. A voiceprint is just as unique as a fingerprint. Some security systems are set up to accept a person's voiceprint as identification for entry into a secure area. We are complex beings uniquely created with different voices and personalities. When God speaks to your spirit or gives you a vision or something supernatural from Him, don't be afraid to speak it forth. You will know it is from Him because it is not something you would ever think up.

I've got news for you. God uses your voice and personality. Go back and look at how different the prophets in the Bible were. Jeremiah was a crybaby prophesying something like this, "Oh, I say unto My people, if only you would come back to Me." Whereas, Ezekiel was bold and forceful, prophesying like this, "I say unto My people, come back to Me, now!" It is the word of the Lord, but the personality of the prophet is in there. If you speak with a southern accent, when you vocalize the word of the Lord, I guarantee it is going to come out in a southern accent. God uses our uniqueness and beautifully blends the "natural" and the "super" to make something supernatural.

I listened to a preacher that had the worst grammar I've ever heard, give the word of the Lord in a service. He said, "Yeah, I say to you all. I'm comin' for a church. A church that I love, and I'm gonna tell you all. I'm gonna lift you up at that sound of the trumpet. You're gonna see the tops of the trees on the bottoms of your feet." It was one of the most beautiful prophecies of the catching away of the Church I've ever heard, delivered with the worst grammar, but I felt the Spirit of the Lord through that word.

Discerning The Real Thing

Since we know Satan is the father of lies and counterfeits everything God does, we must always use wisdom to discern truth from deception as Jesus told us in this Scripture:

> **For false Christs and false prophets will appear and perform great signs and miracles to deceive even the elect-if that were possible.**
>
> **—Matthew 24:24 (NIV)**

In his powerful book, *The Call,* Rick Joyner spoke of discerning the true from the false. Let's read a brief excerpt from his introduction:

Jesus warned that in the last days there would be many false prophets (Matthew 24:24). This is to be expected, because as the Lord also taught, whenever He sows wheat in a field, the enemy comes along and sows tares in the same field. Tares look like wheat, may even taste like wheat, but they are noxious.

Satan will immediately try to counterfeit everything that God is doing, creating confusion, and if possible, deceiving even the elect. However, Satan could not do this if God did not allow it. Obviously, the Lord wants us to learn to distinguish the real from the false and allow the real to be tested by the false in order to purify that which is true. That false prophets are also becoming more prevalent should not surprise us, but rather, encourage us to seek the real with greater determination. If we do not want to be deceived by the false, the answer is not to reject all prophecy, but rather to know what is true. Those who cannot discern true prophecy in times to come will be increasingly subject to the false. If God is planting something, it is because we need it. If we do not plant a field but rather neglect it, the only harvest reaped will be weeds.[3]

If we don't learn to recognize the voice of God and discern the prophetic voice of God, we will be subject to taking in any old wind of doctrine that comes along. It may be true, it may be false. This is exactly why so many people are being drawn into the rising number of cults we are hearing about today, like the Branch Davidians in Waco, Texas and the group in California that committed mass suicide. When you know THE TRUTH — Jesus Christ — and hear His voice, you will recognize what is false. Sheep know the Shepherd's voice after they have heard Him speak and developed an intimacy with Him.

Prophecy is important and God doesn't want us to miss or reject what He is saying to us in these perilous times. That's why we are going to spend some time in the final chapter of this book discussing how to listen to the *real* voice of God, and how to confirm a true prophetic word by applying a checklist.

Chapter 20

How Can I Know It's You, Lord?

If Jesus was standing in front of you in the flesh and you could ask Him just one question, what would it be? Would you ask Him something about His will for your life or about your future, or about how to pray for a miracle in the life of a loved one or yourself? Whatever question you had for Him, just think what it would be like to hear His physical voice speak of something close to your heart.

We all face things in life we don't understand and need the answers to our questions that only He can provide. We need direction from Him to help us turn the desires of our hearts into realities. That is why hearing the voice of God is such a necessary component of our spiritual walk. The three keys to hearing His voice are:

1. *Desiring to hear His voice*

2. *Believing you can hear Him*

3. *Finding out how to hear and know it is Him*

This pattern of desiring, believing, and finding out how to do it, has been repeated in many biblical stories. Naaman, a captain in the king's army, was a leper who desperately wanted to be healed. He needed a word from the Lord and was told by a servant about a prophet of the Lord that lived in Israel. He went to see the prophet to find out what he needed to do to be healed. The prophet Elisha sent his assistant out to tell Naaman to go dip seven times in the Jordan River, and he would be healed.

Naaman was not impressed. In fact he went away angry. First of all, he was insulted that Elisha didn't come speak to him directly. After all, he was a man of authority. Secondly, the Jordan River was a stinking muddy excuse for a river, and he probably felt it was beneath his dignity to be seen bathing at such a place.

Too many times people think they have to go to the big-named evangelist or prophet to get a word from the Lord. They want to see the head guy. Then they want to second-guess God's ways.

A few years ago, a man who was in the hospital called and asked to have the pastor come pray for his healing. I talked with the man on the phone and said, "We have healing teams that can come and minister to you and get you healed."

"I don't want any second class bunch, I want the head cheese!"

"You want me to come and pray for you?"

"Either you come here and pray for me or I don't want anybody."

"Okay, I'll come pray for you."

I went to the hospital and prayed for the man. Later I received word that he had died, and the thought came to me that if he had allowed our healing team to come, he would have been touched by God and healed. Pride goes before the fall.

Naaman's servants spoke some truth in love to him and convinced him to do what the prophet had instructed him to do. When he obeyed and went down into the Jordan River, reluctantly I'm sure, he didn't just dip three or four times. He followed through with the instructions and the seventh time when he came out of the water his skin was as smooth and clean as a baby's skin. The leprosy, an incurable, dreaded disease, was gone.

I have known sick or afflicted people who would go to a healing meeting with no results, but they didn't stop going back again and again and again until a rhema word from the Lord penetrated their hearts. With that word, they knew exactly what to do to receive from God what they needed.

Liz Manns received a rhema word from a prophet of the Lord that told her what to do when Jasmine, her little daughter, was dying from seizures and strokes. Today Jasmine is jumping, leaping, praising, singing and glorifying the Lord in every way.

It is wonderful to hear from the Lord and see a child healed or blind eyes opened by the power of God. It is exciting to hear a prophetic word given to a woman who has been barren for nine years that she will have the child she has been asking of the Lord, and nine months later she delivers that child. Don't you want to be in a place like that to hear prophetic words given and see the miraculous results?

Truth Or Consequences?

When seeking a prophetic word from the Lord through a human vessel, we must be aware it is a matter of truth or consequences. There are times when people speak in the name of the Lord, but they are actually speaking out of their own imaginations. They may be sincere in their intent, but they are deceived into thinking they are hearing the Lord's voice. If you receive a word that is not from the Lord, it will have a detrimental affect on you. It can cause your work to be worthless and put a curse on your life. Those are serious consequences.

I have known people that have quit their jobs and launched into a ministry God had not called them to because a prophet told them they were going to be raised up as a missionary to a certain place. I have seen them lose their credibility and walk in darkness for years because of a word from a prophet who was speaking out of his own imagination.

Jeremiah faced the same thing in his day. There were true prophets and false prophets. Here is my paraphrase of what Jeremiah was telling the people. He said, "Look, you're going into captivity in Babylon because of the sins of the nation. And you are going to be there a long time, so I want you to build your houses, have children and grandchildren, plant your gardens and support King Nebuchadnezzar. I want you to pray for the peace and prosperity of Babylon because as long as Babylon experiences peace and prosperity, you are going to have peace and prosperity right along with it. But if you rebel, there is going to be trouble."

The false prophets came along and said, "Don't listen to Jeremiah. He's prophesying gloom and doom. God loves His people and is not that concerned about their sins. In fact, within two years, you are going to be released from Babylon and the yoke is going to be broken." This was what the people of Israel wanted to hear, and they ran after it instead of listening to Jeremiah.

Then Jeremiah said, "Okay, you had a wooden yoke over your neck. You think you're only going to be there two years so you aren't building houses, planting gardens or having children and grandchildren. You aren't doing what the Lord said to do because you're only planning to stay there a little while. God said now an iron yoke is going to come around your neck." What Jeremiah prophesied is exactly what happened to the people of Israel.

Jeremiah was a true prophet and made it into the Bible. None of those other false prophets have their own book in the Bible. It is pretty clear what the Lord thinks of people who speak out of their own imaginations as He tells us in this Scripture:

> Do not listen to the words of the prophets who prophesy to you. They make you worthless; they speak a vision of their own heart, not from the mouth of the Lord.
>
> —Jeremiah 23:16

Words spoken by false prophets will make you worthless and of no value.

Ezekiel devotes an entire chapter to the subject of false prophets and false prophecy. I want to focus on this one verse:

> They have envisioned futility and false divination, saying, 'Thus says the LORD!' But the LORD has not sent them; yet they hope that the word may be confirmed.
>
> —Ezekiel 13:6

Too many Christians run around from meeting to meeting, pastor-to-pastor or prophet-to-prophet, trying to get someone to confirm what they think the Lord wants them to do, when what they are doing isn't the Lord's plan at all. Let me tell you, if you look far enough you'll find someone to confirm it, but it won't be prophecy from the Lord. It will be divination, and it will release a curse over your household and over your life.

Beware Of Jezebel!

Divination is an imitation of the divine. Believe me, you don't want an imitation when you can have the *real* thing. I have literally seen churches and ministries destroyed by a self-appointed, false prophet or prophetess that comes in imparting instruction and manipulating the leadership to do what he or she says to do. It opens the door to a seducing spirit that causes people to stray unaware and commit spiritual fornication, which is running after something other than God. This is the Jezebel spirit of which the apostle John warned the church in Thyatira in this Scripture:

> "I know your works, love, service, faith, and your patience; and *as* for your works, the last *are* more than the first. Nevertheless I have a few things against you, because you allow that woman Jezebel, who calls herself a prophetess, to teach and seduce My servants to commit sexual immorality and eat things sacrificed to idols. And I gave her time to repent of her sexual immorality, and she did not repent. Indeed I will cast her into a sickbed, and those who commit adultery with her into great tribulation, unless they repent of their deeds. I will kill her children with death, and all the churches shall know that I am He who searches the minds and hearts. And I will give to each one of you according to your works."
>
> —Revelation 2:19-23

Who is this Jezebel? She was a "self-appointed" prophetess. She wasn't sent by God or recognized by the pastor. She probably came in with a printed business card displaying the title, "Prophetess." I have seen people do this, and I run the other direction when I see it. God isn't into titles. A true prophet or prophetess doesn't have to announce what they are. In fact, the ones I know are so humble they won't ever make such a proclamation.

The sign of a Jezebel spirit being in operation is when you see manipulation and seduction causing people to stray away from God rather than being drawn to God. When you see a person's life straying, I guarantee they have gotten a false word somewhere. It may have come from a false prophet or from a false word in something they have read.

This church of Thyatira was very much alive and doing good works of love and faithful service until it allowed this Jezebel prophetess to come in and give instruction to God's people. They were seduced, and didn't even know it was happening.

It is a serious matter to speak in the name of the Lord. When we listen to the *real* voice of God, we will be effective, fruitful and productive in what we do for Him. I don't want you to fear prophecy just because there are false prophets, but rather to be wise in judging what you hear. I want you to experience all of the wonderful benefits of hearing God's voice.

Test The Word

Here is a checklist to help you determine if a word of prophecy is from the Lord whether it comes through a prophet, a dream or vision, an inner voice or urging, or a revelation of the Word of God:

• *Does it exhort, strengthen or comfort you?*

Based on 1 Corinthians 14:3, the real purpose of prophecy is to edify, exhort and build up as we discussed in the last chapter. Jesus did not come to condemn the world but to give us life.

• *What is the spirit behind the prophecy?*

Just because a word is spoken in church doesn't mean it is being given in the right spirit. We are instructed to test the spirits to determine whether they are of God or not, as it says in this Scripture:

> Dear friends, do not believe every spirit, but test the spirits to see whether they are from God, because many false prophets have gone out into the world. This is how you can recognize the Spirit of God: Every spirit that acknowledges that Jesus Christ has come in the flesh is from God, but every spirit that does not acknowledge Jesus is not from God. This is the spirit of the antichrist, which you have heard is coming and even now is already in the world.
>
> —1 John 4:1-3 (NIV)

If you want to be sure the word you hear is coming from the Holy Spirit, simply ask this question, "Has Jesus Christ come in the flesh?" If you don't get any answer, you know it is not from God.

Here is an example of how this works. Joe was flying to Colorado and had pulled out his Bible to read a bit during the flight. The Lord spoke to him and said, "I have provided Margie to be your wife!" He was not expecting such a revelation from the Lord at that time and was rightfully cautious about accepting it. He spoke to the spirit and said, "If you can tell me Jesus Christ has come in the flesh, I will accept this word as from the Lord."

The Spirit spoke to him again and said, "Son, Jesus Christ has come in the flesh and I am telling you I have provided Margie to be your wife!"

Joe responded, "Okay, Lord I receive Your word." He spent many hours in prayer and in the Scriptures to be sure the word bore witness before talking with Margie about it. When he did, she confirmed she had received a similar word in a vision from the Lord on the same day the Lord spoke to Joe and had held it in her heart.

They then went to their pastor and submitted the word of the Lord to him for prayer and confirmation. The pastor prayed and had a vision from the Lord. He saw Joe and Margie dressed in battle fatigues standing on a hilltop preparing to go down into the enemy's camp. The pastor gave them his blessing and agreed to perform the wedding ceremony.

Margie and Joe wanted this word confirmed in the mouths of two or three witnesses and did not tell anyone else about what the Lord had told them. One night at church another church leader came up to them and spoke over them that he saw them dressed for battle riding on identical white horses going forth in the name of the Lord. Another couple also shared with them that the Lord had called them to minister as a team. Joe and Margie married and are now ministering deliverance and inner healing to the body of Christ.

• *Does it conform with Scripture?*

God has given us His written Word as a plumb line and instruction manual for life. If a word you hear doesn't line up with what the Scripture teaches, it doesn't pass the test. Here is an example of how people get drawn off course by their own fleshly desires.

Martha, who was unhappily married to an unbeliever, was talking to another woman at church and said, "I'd like to praise the Lord because I'm getting married."

The woman noticed that Martha was already wearing a wedding ring and said, "But I thought you were already married."

"Yes, I am, but God is going to get rid of him. He doesn't treat me right, and God said I am going to marry a man named Chris."

"Do you mean to tell me you want your husband to die? He's not saved and will go to hell without Christ. Do you want him to be in hell for eternity?"

Martha broke into tears and realized it was her own desire to be free from the unhappy life she was living that caused her to be deceived. God will not speak anything that doesn't line up with His Word.[1]

• *Does it display the character of Christ?*

Sometimes wolves in sheep's clothing will manipulate God's Word for their own advantage. They come into church and start gathering disciples away from the flock. They can't seem to connect in any of the regular church prayer meetings, mission groups or Bible studies. They have to have their own little group, so they begin having their own "informal" Bible studies in their home, inviting just a select few to attend.

There isn't any reason to burden the pastor with it. They tell the little flock not to mention it to anyone else at church because there really isn't room to have any more come right now, and they don't want anyone's feelings to be hurt. The teaching gets weirder and weirder, and eventually the group splits off from the church.

I've seen sheep get picked off like flies by such a tactic. It breaks my heart when that happens. The people who are drawn away are too immature to recognize the true character of the person that is luring them away from the safety of the flock.

• *Is it manipulative in nature?*

Manipulation is a fruit of the spirit of divination. It masquerades in many subtle forms to get you to do what the person speaking the word wants you to do. I may need someone to help with the bus ministry but if I start manipulating you in the name of the Lord to drive the bus, I've gone too far. It's not God. The Lord has to put it on your heart to drive the bus or your ministry will be worthless and ineffective.

• *Does it usurp the gifts or desires God puts on your heart?*

A young minister went to a prophetic conference. Things had been pretty rough in his ministry and he was feeling it might be time to make a change in his life. A prophetess at the conference called him out for a word. She said, "God has raised you up as an engineer and is going to use you in the field of engineering."

This guy was a ditz when it came to math but loved the concept of engineering. He left his ministry and went to college to become an engineer. After all, he could build bridges in foreign nations and share the Gospel with people while he was there.

After about a year and a half his life began to fall apart. He lost a lot of money and time and started getting really cold toward the Lord. Another young minister friend on staff at a large church in the area called this "wannabe" engineer on the phone one day and said, "Look, I'm going to tell you something. I don't care what that prophetess said to you. You are not called to be an engineer. You are called to ministry and that is where God wants you to be. It is time to get your life back together and get back into the ministry. The gifts and callings of God are irrevocable. You are a pastor not an engineer."

The young man repented, turned his life around, and today is serving God as an associate pastor in California. He had to reject the word that didn't line up with the gifts and desires God had put on his heart.

• *Does it pull rank or circumvent authority?*

God's Word tells us to honor authority. When someone elevates his or her prophetic calling to a level that circumvents the godly authority of the church, he or she is not being used of God.

A pastor at a large church began noticing a man who always sat in the front row taking notes during the sermon, and worshipping intensely during praise and worship. He seemed to be really involved in spiritual things. However, the pastor just had a funny feeling about this man. It seemed like everybody this man ministered to ended up leaving the church.

At a staff meeting one day the pastor said, "Look, I don't know what there is about this man. Everything looks good on the outside. He worships and studies and 'amens.' He does all the right stuff but something just isn't right. Every life he touches seems to be ruined."

The pastor asked two of his associates to look into the matter. They decided to fast and pray about it separately before meeting with the man. During prayer one associate pastor prayed, "Lord, everything looks right with this man. He seems to be anointed, but it seems like the lives he ministers to end up falling apart. What is the problem?"

The Lord said, "The man thinks he is a prophet."

The next time the associate pastor saw this man he pulled him aside and said, "Let me ask you a question. Do you think you are a prophet?"

"Yes, I'm a prophet. I've been to some of the big prophetic meetings, and I'm a prophet!"

"One of the other associate pastors and I would like to meet with you."

They arranged a meeting and during the discussion, the man said, "Yes, I am a prophet. I have insight from God that the pastor doesn't have."

The two pastors had to speak some truth in love to this man. They said, "Brother, you are in rebellion to the authority in this church. You are ministering divination evidenced by the fact that the lives of those to whom you are ministering seem to be falling apart and leaving the church."

The man reluctantly agreed to stop ministering the way he had been doing. It wasn't long before he left the church saying he was going to become a nationally known prophet. He got into some kind of trouble, was arrested and spent time in jail. He later beat up his wife and ended up with a divorce, losing his family and his ministry. His prophecies were coming out of his own imagination and not from God. It was spiritual witchcraft, and it brought a curse on his life. It also damaged the lives of those to whom he ministered. Pride stepped in and made him feel he was a step above the pastor because he was "a prophet!"

• *Does it allow outside perspective?*

If anyone tries to tell you not to communicate the word you have been given to anyone else, watch out. One of the tactics of the devil is secrecy. This doesn't mean you have to tell just anybody about what the Lord is saying to you. Any word that affects important decisions in your life should be carefully weighed and confirmed. Are you willing to go to the elders or the pastor to seek their insight and confirmation? It is for your protection and good benefit to do so.

In the earlier example about testing the spirits, Joe and Margie were careful to go to their pastor for prayer and confirmation. They submitted themselves to his authority and were willing to receive his counsel if he disagreed with what they thought they had heard. This was wisdom.

• *Does it produce good fruit in your life and does it come to pass?*

A word from the Lord will only produce good fruit in your life. Does it bring joy and peace? God won't lead you into something you hate doing. If the word is from the Lord it should bring satisfaction and enjoyment. That is a good test of whether a word is from the Lord.

A prophetess once prophesied over a pastor's three children. To one she said, "You are going to be a pastor and have a wonderful church." To another she said, "You are going to be a pilot and fly missionaries to different countries." Then prophesying to the daughter who was just getting ready to go to college, she said, "Don't get a summer job this year because God is going to provide everything for you. People are going to bring money to you. You won't need a job this summer."

The oldest son went off to Bible College and hated it. He felt no call to be a pastor and struggled through a two or three semesters before he came to his dad and said, "Dad, we've got to talk. I know that woman said I was supposed to be a pastor, but I don't like Bible School. I love the Lord and His Word but you know I've always wanted to do something else."

His father was in agreement and said, "Son, that bears witness with me. We need to reject that prophecy."

The other son worked hard and saved up all of his money to take flying lessons to get his pilot's license. Every time he went up he got airsick and would throw up. He hated it and was petrified of flying. Finally, he came to his dad and said, "Dad, I know the prophetess said I was supposed to be a pilot and carry missionaries around, but I hate it. Can I quit?"

Again, the father said, "I bear witness to that. Yes, son you can quit taking flying lessons."

The real trouble came with the daughter. The family had a strong work ethic. When the prophetess told her not to work, she simply lazed around doing nothing. And no money came dropping out of the sky. Her father finally said to her, "Honey, I think you need to get a job. We made a mistake bringing that prophetess to our church." His daughter's response shocked him.

"I'm not going to get a job. I'm going to obey God, not you!" She got into rebellion that lasted a number of years before she accepted that the word was not a true prophecy, just because it came as a "Thus saith the Lord . . .."

A word should always be tested by the fruit it produces. If the fruit is frustration, confusion or rebellion, you know it doesn't pass the test. As far as whether the word actually comes to pass, you must keep in mind God's timing is not always our timing. Consider how many years it took for Joseph's dream to be fulfilled. However, if it never comes to pass, the prophet may have spoken presumptuously as it says in this Scripture:

> You may say to yourselves, "How can we know when a message has not been spoken by the LORD?" If what a prophet proclaims in the name of the LORD does not take place or come true, that is a message the LORD has not spoken. That prophet has spoken presumptuously. Do not be afraid of him.
>
> — Deuteronomy 18:21,22 (NIV)

Use this checklist to help identify the voice of the Lord. The more you practice listening and discerning His voice, the sharper your spiritual senses will be. Don't be afraid of missing it once in a while. We are all human. Just know that if you seek the Lord, you will find Him. If you ask, He will answer. And if you knock, He will open the door to His heart. He loves you and He wants to talk with you.

If you listen to the Holy Spirit, He will guide you into all truth. You are going to have an adventure of a lifetime listening to the Lord, hearing from the Lord, and following the Lord. Your life will be prosperous, not worthless. Your family will be blessed, not cursed. Have you heard from the Lord lately?

"We must trust God with our very lives and then step out in faith believing that His promises are true."

Conclusion

God Holds The Answer To Your Future

I pray that after reading this book you have gained a deeper revelation and understanding of what Jesus did for you on the Cross, and the role the Holy Spirit can play in your daily life if you embrace what He has to offer. He is here to comfort and guide you and to tell you things to come. He holds the answer to your future. It's up to you to determine what you get out of it and how you impact others around you, depending on your willingness to submit to God.

Joseph Garlington, an author, a gifted worshiper and anointed prophetic voice for our times says we must stand "under" before we can understand. In other words, we must submit all that we are and all that we have to God - stand under His authority -

before He will give us the understanding of where He is taking us. We must trust Him with our very lives, and then step out in faith believing that His promises are true.

The days and times in which we are living are the most exciting and perhaps the most perilous of all the ages. If we tune our ears to hear His voice and do what He tells us to do, our lives will undoubtedly be filled with fascinating adventures.

God's Master Plan for your life is bigger than you can see with normal eyes. How you look at something determines what you see. If you want to discover new ways of seeing and hearing in the spiritual realm, you must stand in His presence, tap into His power, and let Him show you things to come. As you learn to hear His voice and see with spiritual eyes, you will grow in maturity and effectiveness, powerfully impacting the work of His kingdom in this millennium.

Endnotes

Introduction
1Mike Bickle, p. 39-40.

Chapter 1
1Chuck Smith, Word For Today Cassette "Word Of Knowledge."

2C. Peter Wagner, <u>Signs and Wonders Today</u>.

Chapter 2
1Prayer and Spiritual Warfare Video Seminar Series, Global Harvest Ministries, Gospel Light Video.

2John Howie, <u>Scots Worthies</u>, p. 27.

3Jack Deere, <u>Surprised by the Voice of God</u>, p. 79.

4C. Peter Wagner, <u>Spreading the Fire</u>, p. 9.

Chapter 3
1Jack Deere, p. 65.

2Ibid, p. 66.

3Bob Mumford. p. 44-45..

4Prayer and Spiritual Warfare Video Seminar Series, Global Harvest Ministries, Gospel Light Video.

Chapter 4
1Steve Blow

2Jeffrey Weiss

3Ibid.

4Chuck Pierce sermon.

Chapter 5
1J. Lynn Lunsford.

2Ibid.

Chapter 6
1Brigid Schulte.

2Ibid.

Chapter 7
1John Howie, p. 28.
Chapter 8
1Bob Mumford, p. 163.
Chapter 9
1Biblesoft's New Exhaustive Strong's.
Chapter 10
1Biblesoft's New Unger's Dictionary.
Chapter 11
1Terry Moore.

2Biblesoft's New Exhaustive Strong's.

3Ibid.

4Brown Driver & Briggs Hebrew Lexicon.
Chapter 12
1Charles H. Spurgeon, p. 226-227.

2Ibid.

3Cheryl and Harry Salem, p. 14-16.

4Ibid, p. 21.
Chapter 13
1Jane Rumph, p. 66-67.

2Ibid.

3James Robison, p. 15.

4Ibid, p. 98.

5Cindy Jacobs, p. 84.

6Jack Deere, p.16-17

7Ibid.

8Cindy Jacobs, p. 30.

9Ibid.
Chapter 14
1Keith Hulen, p. 5.

Chapter 15

1James Ryle, p. 53-54.

2James Ryle, p. 26.

3Paul Yonggi Cho, p. 11-12.

4Ibid, p. 17.

Chapter 16

1Cindy Jacobs, p. 220.

2Jack Taylor.

3Carl Mendera, "The Mission to the Muslims.".

43Ibid..

5Cindy Jacobs, p. 211.

6Ibid, p. 213-214.

7James Ryle, p. 52.].

Chapter 17

1Cindy Jacobs, p. 212.

2James Ryle, p. 69.

3Paul Cain, Morningstar Cassette, "Winds Of Fire,"

Chapter 18

1Biblesoft's New Exhaustive Strong's.

2Jane Rumph, p. 68-69.

3Ibid, p.78-81.

Chapter 19

1Chuck Pierce, GI News, p. 6-7.

2Rick Joyner, p. 13.

Chapter 20

1Cindy Jacobs, p. 74-75.

Conclusion

1Joseph Garlington.

References

Biblesoft's New Exhaustive Strong's Number and Concordance with Expanded Greek-Hebrew Dictionary. Biblesoft and International Translators, Inc. 1994.

Bickle, Mike. Growing in the Prophetic. Lake Mary, FL: Creation House. 1996.

Blow, Steve. "Sex Addiction Shouldn't be Kept Closeted," Dallas Morning News. March 5, 2000.

Cho, Paul Yonggi. The Fourth Dimension. South Plainfield, NJ: Bridge Publishing, Inc. 1979.

Deere, Jack. Surprised by the Voice of God. Grand Rapids, MI: Zondervan Publishing House. 1996.

From the On-line Bible Brown Driver & Briggs Hebrew Lexicon. Ontario, Canada from the Institute for Creation Research: Woodside Bible Fellowship. 1993.

Garlington, Joseph. Sermon tape. Sojourn Church, Carrollton, TX. July 1, 2000.

Howie, John. Scots Worthies. ed. William McGavin. Glasgow: W.R. McPhun. 1846.

Hulen, Keith. "Can My Mommy See Me?" Dallas, TX: Christ for the Nations Magazine. March 5, 2000.

Jacobs, Cindy. The Voice of God. Ventura, CA: Regal Books. 1995.

Joyner, Rick. <u>The Call</u>. Charlotte, NC: Morningstar. 1999.

Lunsford, J. Lynn. "Variables Stacked Against Pilot, Experts say." <u>Dallas Morning News.</u> July 18, 1999.

Menderas, Carl. "The Mission to the Muslims." Testimony tape. Boulder Valley Vineyard, Longmont, CO.

Moore, Terry. Sermon @ Sojourn Church, Carrollton, TX. June 11, 2000.

Mumford, Bob. <u>Take Another Look at Guidance.</u> Raleigh, NC: Lifechangers Publishing. 1993.

Pierce, Chuck. Sermon @ Sojourn Church: Carrollton, TX. November 19, 1999.

Pierce, Chuck. "Unlocking Wealth: Diaries of a Strategic Prayer Journal." <u>GI News.</u> Vol. 9, #2. June/July 2000.

Robison, James. <u>My Father's Face.</u> Sisters, OR: Multnomah Books. 1997.

Rumph, Jane. <u>Stories for the Front Lines.</u> Grand Rapids, MI: Chosen Books. 1996.

Salem, Cheryl and Harry. <u>An Angel's Touch</u>. Tulsa, OK: Harrison House. 1997.

Schulte, Brigid. "A Painful Lesson: Middle-school Students Facing Harsh Realities After Fabricating Story About Teacher." <u>Dallas Morning News.</u> March 25, 2000.

Spurgeon, Charles H. The Autobiography of Charles Spurgeon. Curts & Jennings. 1899. Vol. II.

Taylor, Jack. The Hallelujah Factor. Nashville, TN: Broadman Press. 1983.

Wagner, C. Peter. Signs and Wonders.

Wagner, C. Peter, Spreading the Fire. Ventura, CA: Regal Books. 1994.

Weiss, Jeffrey. "Nowhere to Run: Violence Moving to Places Once Considered Safe." Dallas Morning News. September 16, 1999.

Suggested Reading

Bickle, Mike. Growing in the Prophetic. Lake Mary, FL: Creation House. 1996.

Deere, Jack. Surprised by the Voice of God. Grand Rapids, MI: Zondervan Publishing House. 1996.

Hamon, Bill Dr. Prophets and Personal Prophecy. Shippensburg, PA: Destiny Image Publishers, Inc. 1987.

Hamon, Bill Dr. Apostles Prophets and the Coming Moves of God. Shippenburg, PA: Destiny Image Publisher, Inc. 1997.

Heflin, Wallace H. Jr.. Hear the Voice of God. Hagerstown, MD: McDougal Publishing. 1997.

Jacobs, Cindy. The Voice of God. Ventura, CA: Regal Books. 1995.

Joyner, Rick. The Call. Charlotte, NC: Morningstar. 1999.

Mumford, Bob. Take Another Look at Guidance. Raleigh, NC: Lifechangers Publishing. 1993.

Ryle, James. A Dream Come True. Lake Mary, FL: Creation House. 1995.

Rumph, Jane. Stories for the Front Lines. Grand Rapids, MI: Chosen Books. 1996.

Salem, Cheryl and Harry. An Angel's Touch. Tulsa, OK: Harrison House. 1997.

Thomas, Benny. Exploring the World of Dreams. Springdale, PA: Whitaker House. 1990.

About The Author

Dave Williams is pastor of Mount Hope Church and International Outreach Ministries, with world headquarters in Lansing, Michigan. He has served for over 20 years, leading the church in Lansing from 226 to over 4000 today. Dave sends trained ministers into unreached cities to establish disciple-making churches, and, as a result, today has "branch" churches in the United States, Philippines, and in Africa.

Dave is the founder and president of Mount Hope Bible Training Institute, a fully accredited institute for training ministers and lay people for the work of the ministry. He has authored 45 books including the fifteen-time best seller, *The Start of Something Wonderful* (with over 2,000,000 books sold), and more recently, *The Miracle Results of Fasting*, and *The Road To Radical Riches*.

The Pacesetter's Path telecast is Dave's weekly television program seen over a syndicated network of secular stations, and nationally over the Sky Angel satellite system. Dave has produced over 125 audio cassette programs including the nationally acclaimed *School of Pacesetting Leadership* which is being used as a training program in churches around the United States, and in Bible Schools in South Africa and the Philippines. He is a popular speaker at conferences, seminars, and conventions. His speaking ministry has taken him across America, Africa, Europe, Asia, and other parts of the world.

Along with his wife, Mary Jo, Dave established The Dave and Mary Jo Williams Charitable Mission (Strategic Global Mission), a mission's ministry for providing scholarships to pioneer pastors and grants to inner-city children's ministries.

Dave's articles and reviews have appeared in national magazines such as *Advance, The Pentecostal Evangel, Ministries Today, The Lansing Magazine, The Detroit Free Press* and others. Dave, as a private pilot, flies for fun. He is married, has two grown children, and lives in Delta Township, Michigan.

You may write to Pastor Dave Williams:

P.O. Box 80825

Lansing, MI 48908-0825

Please include your special prayer requests when you write, or you may call the Mount Hope Global Prayer Center anytime: (517) 327-PRAY

DECAPOLIS
PUBLISHING

For a catalog of products, call:

1-517-321-2780 or

1-800-888-7284

or visit us on the web at:

www.mounthopechurch.org

For Your Spiritual Growth

Here's the help you need for your spiritual journey. These books will encourage you, and give you guidance as you seek to draw close to Jesus and learn of Him. Prepare yourself for fantastic growth!

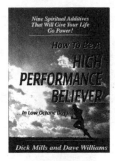

HOW TO BE A HIGH PERFORMANCE BELIEVER
Pour in the nine spiritual additives for real power in your Christian life.

SECRET OF POWER WITH GOD
Tap into the real power with God; the power of prayer. It will change your life!

THE NEW LIFE ...
You can get off to a great start on your exciting life with Jesus! Prepare for something wonderful.

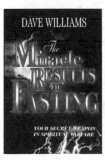

MIRACLE RESULTS OF FASTING
You can receive MIRACLE benefits, spiritually and physically, with this practical Christian discipline.

WHAT TO DO IF YOU MISS THE RAPTURE
If you miss the Rapture, there may still be hope, but you need to follow these clear survival tactics.

THE AIDS PLAGUE
Is there hope? Yes, but only Jesus can bring a total and lasting cure to AIDS.

These and other books available from Dave Williams and:

DECAPOLIS
PUBLISHING

For Your Spiritual Growth

Here's the help you need for your spiritual journey. These books will encourage you, and give you guidance as you seek to draw close to Jesus and learn of Him. Prepare yourself for fantastic growth!

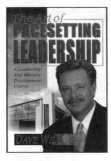

THE ART OF PACESETTING LEADERSHIP
You can become a successful leader with this proven leadership development course.

GIFTS THAT SHAPE YOUR LIFE
Learn which ministry best fits you, and discover your God-given personality gifts, as well as the gifts of others.

GROWING UP IN OUR FATHER'S FAMILY
You can have a family relationship with your heavenly father. Learn how God cares for you.

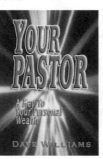

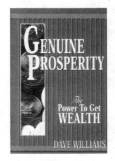

SUPERNATURAL SOULWINNING
How will we reach our family, friends, and neighbors in this short time before Christ's return?

YOUR PASTOR: A KEY TO YOUR PERSONAL WEALTH
By honoring your pastor you can actually be setting yourself up for a financial blessing from God!

GENUINE PROSPERITY
Learn what it means to be truly prosperous! God gives us the power to get wealth!

These and other books available from Dave Williams and:

 DECAPOLIS PUBLISHING

For Your Spiritual Growth

Here's the help you need for your spiritual journey. These books will encourage you, and give you guidance as you seek to draw close to Jesus and learn of Him. Prepare yourself for fantastic growth!

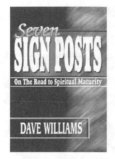

SOMEBODY OUT THERE NEEDS YOU
Along with the gift of salvation comes the great privilege of spreading the gospel of Jesus Christ.

SEVEN SIGNPOSTS TO SPIRITUAL MATURITY
Examine your life to see where you are on the road to spiritual maturity.

THE PASTOR'S PAY
How much is your pastor worth? Who should set his pay? Discover the scriptural guidelines for paying your pastor.

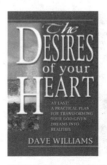

DECEPTION, DELUSION & DESTRUCTION
Recognize spiritual deception and unmask spiritual blindness.

THE ROAD TO RADICAL RICHES
Are you ready to jump from "barely getting by" to Gods plan for putting you on the road to Radical Riches?

THE DESIRES OF YOUR HEART
Yes, Jesus wants to give you the desires of your heart, and make them realities.

These and other books available from Dave Williams and:

DECAPOLIS PUBLISHING

For Your Successful Life

These video cassettes will give you successful principles to apply to your whole life. Each a different topic, and each a fantastic teaching of how living by God's Word can give you total success!

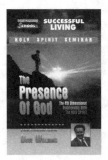  

THE PRESENCE OF GOD
Find out how you can have a more dynamic relationship with the Holy Spirit.

FILLED WITH THE HOLY SPIRIT
You can rejoice and share with others in this wonderful experience of God.

GIFTS THAT CHANGE YOUR WORLD
Learn which ministry best fits you, and discover your God-given personality gifts, as well as the gifts of others.

 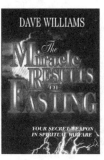 

THE SCHOOL OF PACESETTING LEADERSHIP
Leaders are made, not born. You can become a successful leader with this proven leadership development course.

MIRACLE RESULTS OF FASTING
Fasting is your secret weapon in spiritual warfare. Learn how you'll benefit spiritually and physically! Six video messages.

A SPECIAL LADY
If you feel used and abused, this video will show you how you really are in the eyes of Jesus. You are special!

These and other videos available from Dave Williams and:

DECAPOLIS PUBLISHING

For Your Successful Life

These video cassettes will give you successful principles to apply to your whole life. Each a different topic, and each a fantastic teaching of how living by God's Word can give you total success!

HOW TO BE A HIGH PERFORMANCE BELIEVER
Pour in the nine spiritual additives for real power in your Christian life.

THE UGLY WORMS OF JUDGMENT
Recognizing the decay of judgment in your life is your first step back into God's fullness.

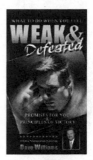

WHAT TO DO WHEN YOU FEEL WEAK AND DEFEATED
Learn about God's plan to bring you out of defeat and into His principles of victory!

WHY SOME ARE NOT HEALED
Discover the obstacles that hold people back from receiving their miracle and how God can help them receive the very best!

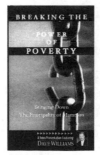

BREAKING THE POWER OF POVERTY
The principality of mammon will try to keep you in poverty. Put God FIRST and watch Him bring you into a wealthy place.

HERBS FOR HEALTH
A look at the concerns and fears of modern medicine. Learn the correct ways to open the doors to your healing.

These and other videos available from Dave Williams and:

DECAPOLIS PUBLISHING

Running Your Race

These simple but powerful audio cassette singles will help give you the edge you need. Run your race to win!

LONELY IN THE MIDST OF A CROWD
Loneliness is a devastating disease. Learn how to trust and count on others to help.

HERBS FOR HEALTH
A look at the concerns and fears of modern medicine. Learn the correct ways to open the doors to your healing.

HOW TO GET ANYTHING YOU WANT
You can learn the way to get anything you want from God!

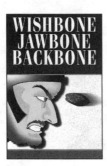

WISHBONE, JAWBONE, BACKBONE
Learn about King David, and how his three "bones" for success can help you in your life quest.

FATAL ENTICEMENTS
Learn how you can avoid the vice-like grip of sin and it's fatal enticements that hold people captive.

HOW TO BE A WALL-BREAKER AND A CITY -TAKER
You can become a powerful force for advancing the Kingdom of Jesus Christ in your community!

These and other audio tapes available from Dave Williams and:

DECAPOLIS PUBLISHING

Expanding Your Faith

These exciting audio teaching series will help you to grow and mature in your walk with Christ. Get ready for amazing new adventures in faith!

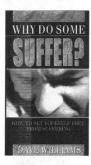

WHY DO SOME SUFFER?
Find out why some people seem to have suffering in their lives, and find out how to avoid it in your life.

SIN'S GRIP
Learn how you can avoid the vice-like grip of sin and it's fatal enticements that hold people captive.

FAITH, HOPE, & LOVE
Listen and let these three "most important things in life" change you.

**PSALM 91
THE PROMISE OF
PROTECTION**
Everyone is looking for protection in these perilous times. God promises protection for those who rest in Him.

**DEVELOPING
THE SPIRIT OF A
CONQUEROR**
You can be a conqueror through Christ! Also, find out how to *keep* those things that you have conquered.

**YOUR SPECTACULAR
MIND**
Identify wrong thinking and negative influences in your life.

These and other audio tapes available from Dave Williams and:

DECAPOLIS PUBLISHING

More Products by Dave Williams

BOOK Title	Price
The New Life — The Start Of Something Wonderful	$1.95
End Times Bible Prophecy	$4.95
Seven Sign Posts On the Road To Spiritual Maturity	$4.95
Somebody Out There Needs You	$4.95
Growing Up In Our Father's Family	$4.95
Grief & Mourning	$7.95
The World Beyond — Mysteries Of Heaven	$7.95
The Secret Of Power With God	$7.95
What To Do If You Miss the Rapture	$9.95
Genuine Prosperity	$9.95
The Miracle Results Of Fasting	$9.95
How To Be A High Performance Believer	$9.95
Gifts That Shape Your Life & Change Your World	$10.95
Road To Radical Riches	$19.95

CD Title	Num. of CDs	Price
Middle East Crisis	1	$12.00
Setting Our Houses In Order	1	$12.00
Too Much Baggage?	1	$12.00
Jesus Loves Sinners	1	$12.00
How To Get Your Breakthrough	1	$12.00
Amazing Power Of Desire	1	$12.00
Wounded Spirit	1	$12.00
The Attack On America (Sept. 11, 2001)	1	$12.00
Radical Wealth	5	$60.00

VIDEO Title	Num. of Videos	Price
What To Do When You Are Going Through Hell	1	$19.95
Acres Of Diamonds — The Valley Of Baca	1	$19.95
120 Elite Warriors	1	$19.95
What To Do If You Miss the Rapture	1	$19.95
Regaining Your Spiritual Momentum	1	$19.95
Herbs For Health	1	$19.95
TheDestructive Power Of Legalism	1	$19.95
4 Ugly Worms Of Judgment	1	$19.95
Grief and Mourning	1	$19.95
Breaking the Power Of Poverty	1	$19.95
Triple Benefits Of Fasting	1	$19.95
Why Some Are Not Healed	2	$39.95
Miracle Results Of Fasting	3	$59.95
ABCs Of Success and Happiness	3	$59.95
Gifts That Shape Your Life and Change Your World	5	$99.95

AUDIO Title	Num. of Tapes	Price
Lonely In the Midst Of a Crowd	1	$6.00
How To Get Anything You Want	1	$6.00
Untangling Your Troubles	2	$12.00
Healing Principles In the Ministry Of Jesus	2	$12.00
Acres Of Diamonds — The Valley Of Baca	2	$12.00
Finding Peace	2	$12.00
Criticize & Judge	2	$12.00
Judgment On America	2	$12.00
Triple Benefits Of Fasting	2	$12.00
Global Confusion	2	$12.00
The Cure For a Broken Heart	2	$12.00
Help! I'm Getting Older	2	$12.00
Regaining Your Spiritual Momentum	2	$12.00
The Destructive Power Of Legalism	2	$12.00
Three Most Important Things In Life	3	$18.00
The Final Series	3	$18.00
The Mysteries of Heaven	3	$18.00
Dave Williams' Crash Course In Intercessory Prayer	3	$18.00
Forgiveness — The Miracle Remedy	4	$24.00
How Long Until the End	4	$24.00
What To Do When You Feel Weak and Defeated	4	$24.00
Sin's Grip	4	$24.00
Why Some Are Not Healed	4	$24.00
Bible Cures	4	$24.00
Belial	4	$24.00
God is Closer Than You Think	5	$30.00
Decoding the Apocalypse	5	$30.00
Winning Your Inner Conflict	5	$30.00
Radical Wealth	5	$30.00
Violent Action For Your Wealth	5	$30.00
The Presence Of God	6	$36.00
Your Spectacular Mind	6	$36.00
The Miracle Results of Fasting	6	$36.00
Developing the Spirit Of a Conqueror	6	$36.00
Why Do Some Suffer	6	$36.00
Overcoming Life's Adversities	6	$36.00
Faith Steps	6	$36.00
ABCs For Success & Happiness	6	$36.00
The Best Of Dave Williams	6	$36.00
How To Help Your Pastor & Church Succeed	8	$48.00
Being a Disciple & Making Disciples	8	$48.00
High Performance Believer	8	$48.00
True Or False	8	$48.00
The End Times	8	$48.00
The Beatitudes — Success 101	8	$48.00
Hearing the Voice Of God	10	$60.00
Gifts That Shape Your Life — Personality Gifts	10	$60.00
Gifts That Shape Your Life & Change Your World — Ministry Gifts	10	$60.00
Daniel Parts 1 & 2 (Both parts 6 tapes each)	12	$72.00
Roadblocks To Your Radical Wealth	12	$72.00
Revelation Parts 1 & 2 (part 1 - 6 tapes; part 2 - 8 tapes)	14	$84.00

Mount Hope Ministries

Mount Hope Missions & International Outreach
Care Ministries, Deaf Ministries
& Support Groups
Access to Christ for the Physically Impaired
Community Outreach Ministries
Mount Hope Youth Ministries
Mount Hope Bible Training Institute
The Hope Store and Decapolis Publishing
The Pacesetter's Path Telecast
The Pastor's Minute Radio Broadcast
Mount Hope Children's Ministry
Champions Club and Sidewalk Sunday School
The Saturday Care Clinic

When you're facing a struggle and need someone
to pray with you, please call us at (517) 321-CARE
or (517) 327-PRAY. We have pastors on duty 24
hours a day. We know you hurt sometimes and
need a pastor, a minister, or a prayer partner. There
will be ministers and prayer partners here for you.

If you'd like to write, we'd be honored to pray for
you. Our address is:

MOUNT HOPE CHURCH
202 S. CREYTS RD.
LANSING, MI 48917
(517) 321-CARE or (517) 321-2780
FAX (517)321-6332
TDD (517) 321-8200

www.mounthopechurch.org
email:
mhc@mounthopechurch.org

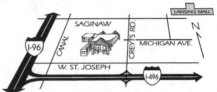

West of the Lansing Mall, on Creyts at Michigan Ave.